A Garland Series

The English Stage
Attack and Defense 1577 - 1730

A collection of 90 important works
reprinted in photo-facsimile in 50 volumes

edited by
Arthur Freeman
Boston University

The Absolute Unlawfulness of the Stage-Entertainment Fully Demonstrated

William Law

The Stage Defended

John Dennis

Law Outlaw'd

Mrs. S. O.

with a preface
for the Garland Edition by

Arthur Freeman

Garland Publishing, Inc., New York & London

1973

Library of Congress Cataloging in Publication Data

Law, William, 1686-1761.
    The absolute unlawfulness of the stage-entertainment
fully demostrated.

    (The English stage: attack and defense, 1577-1730)
    Reprint of 3 works, the 1st printed in 1726 for
W. and J. Innys, London; the 2d printed in 1726 for
N. Blandford, London; and the 3d printed in 1726 for
the benefit of the Candle-Snuffers, London.
    1. Theater--Moral and religious aspects.
I. Dennis, John, 1657-1734. The stage defended.
1973. II. Law outlaw'd. 1973. III. Title.
IV. Series.
PN2047.S7 1973   792'.013   72-170495

    ISBN 0-8240-0632-1

Printed in the United States of America

Preface

Although William Law (1686-1761) is most celebrated for his genial spiritual guidebook, A Serious Call to a Devout and Holy Life *(1728), he was no stranger to theological and philosophical controversy at the time of his diatribe against stage plays. In 1717-19 he had participated vigorously in the Bangorian dispute, assailing Bishop Hoadley in three frequently republished letters; in 1723 he took up cudgels against Mandeville's* Fable of the Bees; *and by 1726 his target was the corrupt and "unlawful" English stage, this in the same year as the amiable* Practical Treatise of Christian Perfection. *Nor was the polemical Law unused to response, response to response, and constant republication: the eighth edition of his first letter to Hoadley (1717) was in print by 1721, and virtually everything he wrote had passed through three separate printings before the bibliographically maddening* Works *of 1753-76.* The Absolute Unlawfulness of the Stage-Entertainments *was no*

5

exception, with at least seven eighteenth-century editions recorded by Lowe-Arnott-Robinson, as well as two different "abridged" and three "slightly abridged" versions — these despite the slim compass of the original. And it is possibly the very brevity of the tract which so recommended it, as well as Law's energetic popular style, for Jeremy Collier's high-handed irony remained undoubtedly "above" a significant proportion of his potentially sympathetic readership. As for its succinct content, The Absolute Unlawfulness *is summarily described by Leslie Stephen as an "uninspired attack upon the stage, which [Law] condemns more unequivocally than Collier, and with less knowledge of the facts," and Hooker finds "in the entire pamphlet . . . not one trace of Law's really keen mind; there is only evidence of a rabid aceticism." We reprint the work from a copy of the first edition in the possession of the publisher, collating A-G⁴. Lowe-Arnott-Robinson 358.*

Law's attack generated no less than three "defences" within the year, one rather pallid Scottish reiteration of 1727, and Allan Ramsay's immediate reaction. Of the replies John Dennis, expectably, provided the most cogent; his The Stage Defended *followed hard upon Law (see*

6

PREFACE

Hooker, ed., Works, *II, 300-321, and notes, II, 508-511). We reprint the British Museum copy (641.e.54), collating* $A^2 a^4 B$-$E^4 F^1$. *Lowe-Arnott-Robinson 370.*

An exceptionally intemperate, if brief, counter-attack by the pseudonymous "Mrs. S——— O———, a lover of both houses," is Law Outlaw'd, *with a facetious London imprint; it excoriates the original polemic in terms even more extreme than Law's own. The "impartial pen" describes Law as a troublesome maniac, who might justly be confined to the Incurable Ward of Bethlehem Hospital. No "Mrs. S——— O———" has been identified, but there may have been intended, erroneously, a mis-attribution to the actress Mrs. Oldfield, whose Christian name "Anne" was not widely known. We reprint this text from the British Museum copy (11794.c.9), collating* A-B⁴. *Lowe-Arnott-Robinson 371.*

May, 1973   A.F.

THE ABSOLUTE

UNLAWFULNESS

OF THE

Stage-Entertainment

FULLY Demonſtrated.

By *WILLIAM LAW*, A. M.

LONDON:

Printed for W. and J. INNYS, at the *Weſt-*
End of St. *Paul's.* MDCCXXVI.

(Price Six-Pence.)

THE

Abſolute Unlawfulneſs

OF THE

STAGE - *Entertainment.*

 Am ſenſible that the Title of this little Book will, to the Generality of People, ſeem too high a Flight; that it will be look'd upon as the Effect of a Fanatical Spirit, carrying Matters higher than the Sobriety of Religion requireth. I have only one Thing to ask of ſuch People, that they will ſuſpend their Judgment for a while, and be content to read ſo ſmall a Treatiſe as this is, before they paſs any judgment either upon the Merits of the Subject, or the Temper of the Writer.

Had a Perſon, ſome Years ago, in the Times of *Popery,* wrote againſt the *Worſhip* of *Images,* as a Worſhip abſolutely unlawful ; our Anceſtors would have look'd upon him as a Man of a very *irregular* Spirit. Now it is poſſible for the preſent Age to be as much miſtaken in their *Pleaſures,* as the

former

former were in their *Devotions* ; and that the allow'd Diverfions of thefe Times may be as great a Contradiction to the
moft Effential Doctrines of Chriftianity, as the *Superftitions*
and *Corruptions* of the former Ages. All therefore that I defire, is only a little *Free-thinking* upon this Subject ; and that
People will not as blindly reject all Reafon, when it examines
their Pleafures, as fome blindly reject all Reafon, when it ex-
mines the Nature of their Devotions.

It is poffible that *fomething* that is called a *Diverfion*, may
be as contrary to the whole Nature of Religion, as any invented Superftition, and perhaps more dangerous to thofe that
comply with it. As the Worfhip of *Images* was a great Sin,
tho' under a Pretence of Piety ; fo the Entertainment of the
Stage may be very finful, tho' it is only intended as a Diverfion.

For if the Worfhip of Images did not ceafe to be finful,
tho' it was intended for pious Purpofes ; it muft be great
Weaknefs to imagine, that the Entertainment of the *Stage*
cannot be any great Sin, becaufe it is only ufed as a Diverfion.

Yet this is a Way of reafoning that a great many People
fall into : They fay, Diverfions are lawful ; that the *Stage* is
only a Diverfion ; that People go to it without meaning any
Harm, and therefore there can be no Sin in it.

But if thefe People were to hear a Man fay, that Religion
is lawful ; that the Worfhip of Images was an Act of Religion ; that he us'd Images as a Means of Religious Devotion,
and therefore there could be no Sin in it : they would mightily lament the Bigotry and Blindnefs of his Mind. Yet furely this is as wife and reafonable, as for a Perfon to fay, I go
to a Play, only as to a Diverfion : I mean no Harm ; and
therefore there can be no Sin in it. For if Practices may be
exceeding finful, tho' they are intended for pious Ends ; certainly Practices may be very abominable, tho' they are only
ufed as Diverfions.

When therefore we condemn the *Blindnefs* of fome Chriftian Countries, for conforming to fuch grofs Corruptions of
Religion, we fhould do well to remember, that they have
thus much to be pleaded in their Excufe, that what they
do, is under a Notion of Piety ; that it is in obedience to
the Authority both of Church and State, and that they are
at the fame time kept entire Strangers to the Scriptures. But
how juftly may the fame Blindnefs be charged upon us, if it
fhould appear, that without having any of their Excufes, our
Pub-

Publick, Stated Diverfions are as contrary to Scripture, and the fundamental Doctrines of Religion, as any of the groffeft Inftances of Superftition? If we hold it lawful to go to wicked, finful Diverfions; we are as great Strangers to True Religion, as they who are pleas'd with buying *Indulgences*, and worfhip Pieces of holy Wood.

For, a *Sinful Diverfion* is the fame Abfurdity in Religion, as a *Corrupt Worfhip*; and it fhews the fame Blindnefs of Mind, and Corruption of Heart, whether we fin againft God in the *Church*, or in our *Clofets*, or in the *Play-Houfe*. If there is any thing contrary to Religion in any of thefe Places, it brings us under the fame Guilt. There may, perhaps, be this difference; that God may be lefs difpleafed with fuch Corruptions as we comply with thro' a blind Devotion, than with fuch as we indulge our felves in thro' a Wantonnefs of Mind, and a Fondnefs for Diverfions.

The Matter therefore ftands thus: If it fhould appear that the Stage-Entertainment is entirely finful; that it is contrary to more Doctrines of Scripture, than the Worfhip of *Images*; then it follows, that all who defend it, and take their Share of it, are in the fame State, as they who worfhip *Images*, and defend Drunkennefs and Intemperance. For, to defend, or fupport any finful Diverfion, is the fame thing as Supporting or Defending any other finful Practice. It therefore as much concerns us to know, whether our Diverfions are reafonable, and conformable to Religion, as to know, whether our Religion be reafonable, and conformable to Truth. For, if we allow our felves in Diverfions that are contrary to Religion, we are in no better a State than thofe, whofe Religion is contrary to Truth.

I have mentioned the Worfhip of *Images*, becaufe it is fo great a Corruption in Religion, fo contrary to Scripture, and fo juftly abhorr'd by all the Reform'd Churches; that the Reader may hence learn what he is to think of himfelf, if the *Stage* is ever his Diverfion: For I am fully perfuaded, that he will here find Arguments againft the *Stage*, as ftrong and plain as any that can be urg'd againft the Worfhip of *Images*, or any other Corruption of the moft corrupt Religion.

Let it therefore be obferv'd, that the Stage is not here condemn'd, as fome other Diverfions, becaufe they are dangerous, and likely to be Occafions of Sin; but that it is condemn'd, as Drunkennefs and Lewdnefs, as Lying and Prophanenefs are to be condemn'd; not as Things that may on-

2

ly be the Occafions of Sin, but as fuch as are in their own Nature grofsly Sinful.

You go to hear a *Play* : I tell you, that you go to hear *Ribaldry* and *Prophanenefs* ; that you entertain your Mind with extravagant Thoughts, wild *Rant*, *blafphemous Speeches*, *wanton Amours*, *prophane Jefts*, and *impure Paffions*. If you ask me, where is the Sin of all this ? You may as well ask me, where is the Sin of *Swearing* and *Lying*. For it is not only a Sin againft this or that particular Text of Scripture, but it is Sin againft the *whole Nature* and Spirit of our Religion.

It is a Contradiction to all Chriftian Holinefs, and to all the Methods of arriving at it. For, can any one think that he has a true Chriftian Spirit; that his Heart is changed as it ought to be; that he is born again of God ; whilft he is diverting himfelf with the Lewdnefs, Impudence, Prophanenefs, and impure Difcourfes of the Stage ? Can he think that he is endeavouring to be holy as Chrift is holy, to live by his Wifdom, and be full of his Spirit, fo long as he allows himfelf in fuch an Entertainment ? For there is nothing in the Nature of Chriftian Holinefs, but what is all contrary to the whole Spirit and Temper of this Entertainment. That Difpofition of Heart, which is to take pleafure in the various Reprefentations of the *Stage*, is as directly contrary to that Difpofition of Heart which Chriftianity requireth, as Revenge is contrary to Meeknefs, or Malice to Good-will. Now that which is thus contrary to the whole Nature and Spirit of Religion, is certainly much more condemned, than that which is only contrary to fome particular Part of it.

But this is plainly the Cafe of the *Stage* : It is an Entertainment that confifts of lewd, impudent, prophane Difcourfes; and, as fuch, is contrary to the *whole Nature* of our Religion. For, all the Parts of Religion, its whole Nature, has only this one Defign ; To give us Purity of Heart, to change the Temper and Tafte of our Souls, and fill us with fuch holy Tempers, as may make us fit to live with God in the Society of pure and glorious Spirits.

An Entertainment therefore which applies to the Corruption of our Nature, which awakens our diforder'd Paffions, and teaches to relifh Lewdnefs, immoral Rant, and Prophanenefs, is exceeding finful ; not only as it is a Breach of fome particular Duty, but as it contradicts the *whole Nature*, and oppofes *every Part* of our Religion.

For

For this Diverfion, which confifts of fuch Difcourfes as thefe, injures us in a very different manner from other Sins. For, as Difcourfes are an Application to our whole Soul, as they entertain the Heart, and awaken and employ all our Paffions; fo they more fatally undo all that Religion has done, than feveral other Sins. For, as Religion confifts in a right Turn of Mind, as it is a State of the Heart; fo whatever fupports a quite contrary Turn of Mind, and State of Heart, has all the Contrariety to Religion that it can poffibly have.

St. *John* faith, *Hereby we know that he abideth in us, by the Spirit which he hath given us.* There is no other certain Sign of our belonging to Chrift; Every other Sign may deceive us: All the External Parts of Religion may be in vain; it is only a State of our Mind and Spirit, that is a certain Proof that we are in a true State of Chriftianity. And the Reafon is plain; becaufe Religion has no other End, than to alter our Spirit, and give us new Difpofitions of Heart, fuitable to its Purity and Holinefs. That therefore which immediately applies to our Spirit, which fupports a wrong Turn of Mind, which betrays our Hearts into impure Delights, deftroys all our Religion; becaufe it deftroys that Turn of Mind and Spirit, which is the fole End and Defign of all our Religion.

When therefore you are asked why it is unlawful to fwear; you can anfwer, becaufe it is contrary to the Third Commandment. But if you are asked, why it is unlawful to ufe the Entertainment of the Stage; you can carry your Anfwer farther; becaufe it is an Entertainment that is contrary to all the Parts, the whole Nature of Religion; and contradicts every holy Temper, which the Spirit of Chriftianity requireth. So that if you live in the ufe of this Diverfion, you have no Grounds to hope, that you have the Spirit and Heart of a Chriftian.

Thus ftands the firft Argument againft the *Stage*: It has all the Weight in it, that the whole Weight of Religion can give to any Argument.

If you are only for the Form of Religion, you may take the Diverfion of the Stage along with it; but if you defire the *Spirit* of Religion, if you defire to be truly religious in Heart and Mind, it is as neceffary to renounce and abhor the Stage, as to feek to God, and pray for the Guidance of his Holy Spirit.

Secondly,

Secondly, Let the next Argument againſt the Stage be taken from its manifeſt Contrariety to this important Paſſage of Scripture. *Let no corrupt communication proceed out of your mouth, but that which is good to the uſe of edifying ; that it may miniſter grace to the hearers : And grieve not the holy Spirit of God, whereby ye are ſealed to the day of redemption.*

Here we ſee, that all corrupt and unedifying Communication is abſolutely ſinful, and forbidden in Scripture for this Reaſon, hecauſe it *grieves the Holy Ghoſt*, and ſeparates *Him* from us. But if it be thus unlawful to have any corrupt Communication of our own; can we think it lawful to go to Places ſet apart for that Purpoſe? To give our Money, and hire Perſons to corrupt our Hearts with ill Diſcourſes, and inflame all the diſorderly Paſſions of our Nature! We have the Authority of Scripture to affirm, that *evil Communication corrupts good Manners*; and that *unedifying Diſcourſes grieve the Holy Spirit.*

Now the *Third* Commandment is not more plain and expreſs againſt *Swearing*, than this Doctrine is plain and poſitive againſt going to the *Play-Houſe*. If you ſhould ſee a Perſon that acknowledges the *Third* Commandment to be a divine Prohibition againſt Swearing ; yet going to a *Houſe*, and giving his *Money* to Perſons, who were there met to *Curſe* and *Swear* in fine Language, and invent *Muſical Oaths and Imprecations*; would you not think him mad in the higheſt degree? Now conſider whether there be a leſs degree of Madneſs in going to the Play-Houſe. You own that God has called you to a great Purity of Converſation ; that you are forbid all *fooliſh Diſcourſe*, and *filthy Jeſtings*, as expreſsly as you are forbid *Swearing* ; that you are told to *let no corrupt Communication proceed out of your mouth, but ſuch as is good for the uſe of edifying :* And yet you go to the *Houſe ſet apart* for corrupt Communications : You hire Perſons to entertain you with all manner of *Ribaldry, Prophaneneſs, Rant,* and *Impurity* of Diſcourſe ; who are to preſent you with *vile* Thoughts, and lewd Imaginations, in *fine Language*, and to make *wicked, vain* and *impure Diſcourſe*, more lively and affecting, than you could poſſibly have it in any ill Company. Now is not this Sinning with as high a Hand, and as groſsly offending againſt plain Doctrines of Scripture, as if you were to give your *Money* to be entertain'd with *Muſical Oaths* and *Curſes* ?

You

You might reasonably think that *Woman* very ridiculous in her *Piety*, that durſt not ſwear her ſelf; but ſhould neverthe-leſs frequent *Places* to hear *Oaths*. But you may as juſtly think her very ridiculous in her *Modeſty*, who, tho' ſhe dares not to ſay, or look, or do an immodeſt Thing her ſelf, ſhould yet give her *Money* to ſee *Women* forget the *Modeſty* of their Sex, and *talk impudently* in a Publick *Play-Houſe*. If the *Play-Houſe* was fill'd with *Rakes*, and *ill Women*, there would be nothing to be wonder'd at in ſuch an Aſſembly : For *ſuch Perſons* to be delighted with ſuch Entertainments, is as natu-ral, as for any *Animal* to delight in its proper *Element*. But for Perſons who profeſs Purity and Holineſs, who would not be ſuſpected of *immodeſt* or *corrupt Communications* ; for them to come under the Roof of a *Houſe devoted* to ſuch ill Pur-poſes, and to be pleaſed Spectators of ſuch Actions and Diſ-courſes, as are the Pleaſures of the moſt abandon'd Perſons ; for them to give their Money to be thus entertain'd. is ſuch a Contradiction to all Piety and common Senſe, as cannot be ſufficiently expoſed.

Conſider now, if you pleaſe, the Worſhip of *Images*. You wonder that any People can be ſo blind, ſo regardleſs of Scripture, as to comply with ſuch a Devotion. It is indeed wonderful. But is it not as wonderful, that you ſhould ſeek and delight in an Entertainment, made up of Lewdneſs, Pro-phaneneſs, and all the extravagant Rant of diſorder'd Paſſi-ons ; when the Scripture poſitively charges you to forbear all *corrupt Communication*, as that which *grieves the Holy Spirit*, and ſeparates him from us ? Is not this being *blind*, and *re-gardleſs* of Scripture in as high a degree ? For how can the Scripture ſpeak higher, or plainer, or enforce its Doctrines with a more dreadful Penalty, than that which is here decla-red ? For, without the Holy Spirit of God, we are but Fi-gures of Chriſtians, and muſt dye in our Sins.

If it was ſaid in Scripture, *Forbear* from all Image-Wor-ſhip, becauſe it *grieves and removes the Holy Spirit* from you; perhaps you would think the Worſhippers of *Images* under greater Blindneſs and Corruption of Heart, than they now are. But, obſerve, that if you go to the *Stage*, you offend againſt Scripture in as high a degree as they, who ſhould worſhip Images, tho' the Scriptures forbid it, as *grievous to the Holy Spirit*.

If therefore I was to reſt here, I might fairly ſay, that I had prov'd the Stage to be as contrary to Scripture, as the Wor-

ſhip

ſhip of *Images* is contrary to the Second Commandment. You think it a ſtrange Contrariety, to ſee People on their Knees before an *Image*, at a Time that the Heart and Mind ſhould raiſe it ſelf to God. But then, is it not as ſtrange a Contrariety, that a Perſon ſhould indulge himſelf in the lewd prophane Diſcourſes of the *Stage*, who ſhould have his Heart and Mind preſerv'd in the Wiſdom, the Purity and Spirit of Religion ? For an Image is not ſo contrary to God, as Plays are contrary to the Wiſdom, the Purity, and the Spirit of Scripture. An Image is only contrary to God, as it has no Power, or Perfection : But *Plays* are contrary to Scripture, as the Devil is contrary to God, as they are full of another Spirit and Temper. He therefore that indulges himſelf in the wicked Temper of the *Stage*, ſins againſt as plain Scripture, and offends againſt more Doctrines of it, than he that uſes *Images* in his Devotions.

I proceed now to a Third Argument againſt the Stage.

When you ſee the *Players* acting with Life and Spirit, Men and Women *equally bold* in all Inſtances of *Prophaneneſs, Paſ-ſion*, and *Immodeſty* ; I dare ſay you never ſuſpect any of them to be Perſons of *Chriſtian Piety*. You cannot, even in your Imagination, join Piety to ſuch Manners, and ſuch a Way of Life. Your Mind will no more allow you to join Piety with the Behaviour of the *Stage*, than it will allow you to think *two* and *two* to be *ten*. And perhaps you had rather ſee your Son chained to a *Galley*, or your Daughter driving *Plow*, than getting their Bread on the *Stage*, by adminiſtring in ſo ſcandalous a manner to the Vices and corrupt Pleaſures of the World. Let this therefore be another Argument, to prove the *Abſolute Unlawfulneſs* of going to a *Play*. For, conſider with your ſelf ; Is the Buſineſs of *Players* ſo contrary to Piety, ſo inconſiſtent with the Spirit and Temper of a true Chriſtian, that it is next to a Contradiction to ſuppoſe them united ? How then can you take your ſelf to be *inno-cent*, who *delight in* their Sins, and *hire* them to commit them ?

You may make your ſelf a Partaker of other Mens Sins, by Negligence, and for want of reproving them : But certainly, if you ſtand by, and aſſiſt Men in their Evil Actions, if you make their Vices your Pleaſures and Entertainment, and pay your Money to be ſo entertain'd ; you make your ſelf a Partaker of their Sins in a very high degree ; and conſequent-ly,

[9]

ly, it muſt be as unlawful to go to a *Play*, as it is unlawful
to approve, encourage, aſſiſt, and reward a Man for *Renouncing* a Chriſtian Life.

Let therefore every *Man*, or *Woman* that goes to a *Play*,
ask themſelves this Queſtion; Whether it ſuits with their Religion, to act the *Parts* that are there acted? Perhaps they
would think this as inconſiſtent with that degree of Piety
that they profeſs; as to do the vileſt Things. But let them
conſider, that it muſt be a wicked and unlawful Pleaſure, to
delight in any thing that they dare not do themſelves. Let
them alſo conſider, that they are really *acting* thoſe *Indecen-
cies* and *Impieties* themſelves, which they think is the particular Guilt of the *Players*. For, a Perſon may very juſtly be
ſaid to do that *himſelf*, which he *pays* for the doing, and
which is done for his Pleaſure.

You muſt therefore, if you would be conſiſtent with your
ſelf, as much abhor the Thoughts of being at a *Play*, as of
being a *Player* your ſelf. For, to think that you muſt forbear the one, and not the other, is as abſurd, as to ſuppoſe,
that you muſt be temperate your ſelf, but may aſſiſt, encourage, and reward other People for their Intemperance. The
Buſineſs of a *Player* is prophane, wicked, lewd and immodeſt: To be any way therefore approving, aſſiſting, or encouraging him in ſuch a way of Life, is as evidently ſinful,
as it is ſinful to aſſiſt and encourage a Man in *Stealing*, or any
other Wickedneſs.

This Argument is not far-fetch'd, or founded in any Sub-
tilties of reaſoning; but is ſo plain and obvious, that the
meaneſt Capacity muſt needs underſtand it. I may venture
to challenge any one to ſhew me, that the Buſineſs of the
Players is a more Chriſtian Employment than that of *Robbers*.
For he muſt know very little of the Nature of Religion, that
can look upon Luſt, Prophaneneſs, and diſorder'd Paſſions, to
be leſs contrary to Religion, than the taking Money from the
right Owner. And a Perſon who devotes himſelf to this Employment, to get his Bread by gratifying the corrupt Taſte of
the World with wanton, wild, prophane Diſcourſes, may be
juſtly ſuppos'd to have a more corrupt Heart himſelf, than
many a Man who has taken unlawful Ways of relieving his
Wants.

I ſpeak to this Matter with thus much Plainneſs, becauſe
there is ſo plain Reaſon for it; and becauſe, I think, there is
as much Juſtice and Tenderneſs in telling every Player, that
his Employment is abominably ſinful, and inconſiſtent with

B 2   the

the Chriftian Religion, as in telling the fame Thing to a *Thief.* As it ought to be reckon'd no Sign of Enmity, or Ill-will, if I fhould attempt to prove to *Malefactors* the horrid Nature of their Sins, and the Neceffity of a fincere Repentance; fo I hope it will not be look'd upon as any Sign of ill Temper, or Anger at any particular Perfons, that I fet the Bufinefs of Players amongft the moft abominable Crimes. For, it is with no other Intent, but that they themfelves may avoid the dreadful Guilt of fo wicked a Profeffion, and that other People may not dare any longer to fupport them in it. For it certainly concerns all People, who are not fo void of Religion as to be Players themfelves, to be ftrictly careful that they have no Share in the Guilt of fo unchriftian a Profeffion.

This we reckon very good Reafoning in all other Cafes. A Perfon that dares not *fteal*, thinks it equally finful to encourage Theft. Any one that abhors *Perjury*, or *Murder*, knows that he commits thofe Sins, if he encourages other People in them. What therefore muft we think of our felves, if the Blafphemy, Prophanenefs, Lewdnefs, Immodefty, and wicked Rant of Plays, are Parts that we dare not act our felves, yet make it our Diverfion to be delighted with thofe that do? Shall we think our felves more enlighten'd, or more reafonable, than thofe that worfhip *Images*? The Second Commandment cannot fright them from the Ufe of Images; but it is becaufe they have had a fuperftitious Education, are taught to be blindly obedient, and have the Pretence of Piety for what they do. But all the groffeft Sins of the *Stage* cannot fright us from it ; tho' we fee the Sins, and have nothing to pretend for Compliance, but mere Idlenefs and Diverfion.

If any one was to collect all the foolifh, vain *Devotions*, which poor miftaken Creatures have paid to *Images*, it would fufficiently juftify our Abhorrence of them, and fhew the Wifdom of the *Reformation* in abolifhing the Ufe of them. But if a Perfon was to make a Collection of all the wicked, prophane, blafphemous, lewd, impudent, deteftable Things, that are faid in the Play-Houfe only in *one Seafon* ; it would appear to be fuch a Mafs of Sin, as would fufficiently juftify any one in faying, that the Bufinefs of Players is the moft wicked and deteftable Profeffion in the World.

All People therefore who ever enter into their Houfe, or contribute the fmalleft Mite towards it, muft look upon themfelves, as having been fo far Friends to the moft powerful

ful Inftruments of Debauchery, and to be guilty of contributing to a bold, open, and publick Exercife of Impudence,
Impurity, and Prophanenefs. When we encourage any good
Defign, either with our Confent, our Money, or Prefence,
we are apt to take a great deal of Merit to our felves; we
prefently conclude, that we are Partakers of all that is *good
and praife-worthy in it*, of all the Benefit that arifes from it,
becaufe we are Contributors towards it. A Man does not
think that he has no Share in fome publick Charity, becaufe
he is but one in ten thoufand that contributes towards it;
but if it be a religious Charity, and attended with great and
happy Effects, his Confcience tells him that he is a Sharer of
of *all* that great Good, to which he contributes. Now let
this teach us, how we ought to judge of the Guilt of encouraging any thing that is bad, either with our *Confent*, our
Money, or our *Prefence*. We muft not confider how much
our fingle Part contributes towards it, nor how much lefs we
contribute than feveral thoufands of other People; but we
muft look at the *whole thing* in it felf, and whatever there is
of Evil in it, or whatever Evil arifes from it, we muft
charge our felves with a Share of the whole Guilt of fo great
an Evil. Thus it is, that we hope, and defire to partake of
the Merit of all good Defigns, which we any way countenance and encourage; and thus it is, that the Guilt of all
wicked things which we countenance and affift, will certainly be laid to our Charge.

To proceed now to a fourth Argument. When I confider *Churches*, and the Matter of *Divine Service*, that it confifts of holy Readings, Prayers, and Exhortations to Piety,
there is Reafon to think, that the Houfe of God is a natural
Means of promoting Piety and Religion, and rendring Men
devout, and fenfible of their Duty to God. The very Nature of Divine Affemblies thus carried on has this direct Tendency: I ask you whether this is not very plain, that *Churches*
thus employ'd fhould have this Effect? Confider therefore the
Play-Houfe, and the Matter of the Entertainment there, as it
confifts of *Love-Intrigues, blafphemous Paffions, prophane Difcourfes, lewd Defcriptions, filthy Jefts*, and all the moft extravagant Rant of wanton, profligate Perfons of both Sexes,
heating and inflaming one another with all the *Wantonnefs* of
Addrefs, the *Immodefty* of Motion, and *Lewdnefs* of Thought,
that Wit can invent: Confider, I fay, whether it be not plain,
that a Houfe fo employed is as certainly ferving the Caufe of

Immo-

Immorality and *Vice*, as the Houfe of God is ferving the Caufe of *Piety*? For what is there in our *Church Service* that fhews it to be *ufeful* to Piety and Holinefs; what is there in Divine Worfhip to correct and amend the Heart, but what is directly contrary to all that is doing in the *Play-Houfe*? So that one may with the fame Affurance affirm, that the *Play-Houfe*, not only when fome very prophane Play is on the *Stage*, but in its *daily, common* Entertainments, is as certainly the *Houfe of the Devil*, as the Church is the *Houfe of God.* For though the Devil be not profeffedly worfhipp'd by Hymns directed to him, yet moft that is there fung is to his Service; he is there *obey'd* and *pleas'd* in as certain a manner, as God is worfhipped and honoured in the Church.

You muft eafily fee, that this Charge againft the *Play-Houfe* is not the Effect of any *particular Temper*, or Weaknefs of Mind; that it is not an *uncertain Conjecture*, or *religious Whimfy*; but is a Judgment founded as plainly in the *Nature* and *Reafon* of things, as when it is affirmed, that the Houfe of God is of Service to Religion: And he that abfolutely condemns the *Play-Houfe*, as wicked and corrupting, proceeds upon as much Truth and Certainty, as he that abfolutely commends the *Houfe of God*, as holy, and tending to promote Piety.

When therefore any one pretends to vindicate the *Stage* to you, as a proper Entertainment for holy and religious Perfons; you ought to reject the Attempt with as much Abhorrence, as if he fhould offer to fhew you, that our *Church Service* was rightly formed for thofe Perfons to join in, who are *devoted to the Devil*. For to talk of the *Lawfulnefs* and *Ufefulnefs* of the *Stage* is full as abfurd, as contrary to the plain Nature of things, as to talk of the Unlawfulnefs and Mifchief of the Service of the Church. He therefore that tells you, that you may fafely go the *Play-Houfe*, as an innocent, ufeful Entertainment of your Mind, commits the fame Offence againft common Senfe, as if he fhould tell you, that it was dangerous to attend at Divine Service, and that its Prayers and Hymns were great *Pollutions* of the Mind.

For the Matter and Manner of *Stage Entertainments* is as undeniable a Proof, and as obvious to common Senfe, that the Houfe belongs to the Devil, and is the Place of his Honour, as the Matter and Manner of *Church Service* proves that the Place is appropriated to God.

Obferve therefore, That as you do not want the Affiftance of any one, to fhew you the *Ufefulnefs* and *Advantage* of
Divine

Divine Service, becaufe the thing is plain, and fpeaks for it felf; fo neither, on the other hand, need you any one to fhew the *Unlawfulnefs* and *Mifchief* of the Stage, becaufe there the thing is equally plain, and fpeaks for it felf. So that you are to confider your felf as having the fame Affurance, that the *Stage* is wicked, and to be abhorred and avoided by all Chriftians, as you have, that the Service of the Church is holy, and to be fought after by all Lovers of Holinefs. Confider therefore, that your Conduct, with relation to the *Stage*, is not a Matter of *Nicety*, or *fcrupulous Exactnefs*; but that you are as certain that you do wrong in as notorious a manner, when you go the *Play-Houfe*, as you are certain that you do right, when you go to *Church*.

Now it is of mighty Ufe to conceive things in a right manner, and to fee them as they are in their own Nature. Whilft you confider the Play-Houfe only as a *Place of Diverfion*, it may perhaps give no Offence to your Mind: There is nothing *fhocking* in the Thought of it; but if you would lay afide this Name of it for awhile, and confider it in its *own Nature*, as it really is, you would find that you are as much deceiv'd, if you confider the *Play-Houfe* as only as *Place of Diverfion*, as you would be, if you confidered the Houfe of God, only as a Place of *Labour*.

When therefore you are tempted to go to a *Play*, either from your own Inclination, or from the Defire of a Friend, fancy that you was asked in plain Terms to go to the Place of the *Devil's Abode*, where he holds his *filthy Court* of evil Spirits; that you was asked to join in an Entertainment, where he was at the Head of it; where the whole of it was in order to his Glory, that Mens Hearts and Minds might be feparated from God, and plunged into all the Pollutions of Sin and Brutality. Fancy that you are going to a Place that as certainly belongs to the Devil, as the *heathen Temples* of old, where *Brutes* were worfhipped, where *wanton Hymns* were fung to *Venus*, and drunken Songs to the God of Wine. Fancy that you was as certainly going to the Devil's *Triumph*, as if you was going to thofe *old Sports*, where People committed Murder, and offered Chriftians to be devoured by wild Beafts, for the Diverfion of the Spectators. Now whilft you confider the *Play-Houfe* in this View, I fuppofe you can no more go to a *Play*, than you can renounce your Chriftianity.

Confi-

Confider now therefore, that you have not been frighting your felf with *groundlefs Imaginations*; but that which you have here fancy'd of the *Play-Houfe* is as ftrictly true, as if you had been fancying, that when you go to Church, you go to the Houfe of God, where the heavenly Hoft attend upon his Service; and that when you read the Scriptures, and fing holy Hymns, you join with the Choirs above, and do God's Will on Earth, as it is done in Heaven. For obferve, I pray you, how juftly that Opinion of the *Play-Houfe* is founded. For was it a Joy to him to fee *Idols* worfhipped, to fee Hymns and Adorations offer'd up to impure and filthy Deities? Were Places and Feftivals appointed for fuch Ends, juftly efteemed Places and Feftivals devoted to the Devil? Now give the Reafon why all this was juftly reckon'd a Service to the Devil, and you will give as good a Reafon, why the *Play-Houfe* is to be efteemed his *Temple*.

For what though Hymns and Adorations are not offer'd to impure and filthy Deities, yet if *Impurity* and *Filthinefs* is the *Entertainment*; if immodeft Songs, prophane Rant, if Luft and Paffion entertain the Audience, the Bufinefs is the fame, and the Affembly does the *fame Honour* to the Devil, though they be not gather'd together in the Name of fome *Heathen God*.

For Impurity and Prophanenefs in the Worfhippers of the True God, is as acceptable a Service to the Devil, as Impurity and Prophanenefs in Idolaters; and perhaps a *lewd Song*, in an Affembly of Chriftians, gives him a greater Delight, than in a Congregation of *Heathens*.

If therefore we may fay, that a *Houfe* or *Feftival* was the Devil's, becaufe he was *delighted* with it; becaufe what was there done, was an *acceptable Service* to him; we may be af-fured, that the *Play-Houfe* is as really the Houfe of the De-vil, as any other Houfe ever was. Nay, it is reafonable to think, that the *Play-Houfes* in this Kingdom are a greater Pleafure to him, than any *Temple* he ever had in the Heathen World. For, as it is a greater Conqueft, to make the Dif-ciples of Chrift delight in *Lewdnefs* and *Prophanenefs*, than ignorant Heathen; fo a *Houfe* that, in the Midft of *Chriftian Churches*, trains up Chriftians to *Lewdnefs* and *Prophanenefs*, that makes the Worfhippers of Chrift flock together in Crowds, to rejoice in an Entertainment that is as contrary to the Spirit of Chrift, as *Hell* is contrary to *Heaven*: A Houfe fo em-ploy'd, may juftly be reckon'd a more delightful Habitation of the Devil, than any Temple in the Heathen World.

When

When therefore you go to the *Play-House*, you have as much Affurance that you go to the Devil's peculiar Habitation, that you fubmit to his Defigns, and rejoice in his Diverfions, (which are his beft Devices againft Chriftianity) you have as much Affurance of this, as that they who worfhipped filthy Deities, were in reality Worfhippers of the Devil.

Hence it appears, that if inftead of confidering the Play-Houfe as only a Place of Diverfion, you will but examine what Materials it is made of; if you will but confider the Nature of the Entertainment, and what is there doing, you will find it as wicked a Place, as finful a Diverfion, and as truly the peculiar Pleafure of the Devil, as any wicked Place, or finful Diverfion in the Heathen World. When therefore you are asked to go to a Play, don't think that you are only asked to go to a Diverfion, but be affured that you are asked to *yield* to the Devil, to go over to his Party, and to make one of his Congregation. That if you do go, you have not only the Guilt of *buying* fo much vain Communication, and paying People for being wicked, but are alfo as certainly guilty of going to the Devil's Houfe, and doing him the fame Honour, as if you was to partake of fome Heathen *Feftival.* You muft confider, that all the Laughter there is not only vain and foolifh, but that it is a Laughter amongft Devils, that you are upon prophane Ground, and hearing Mufick in the very Porch of Hell.

Thus it is in the Reafon of the thing; and if we fhould now confider the State of our *Play-Houfe,* as it is in Fact, we fhould find it anfwering all thefe Characters, and producing Effects fuitable to its Nature. But I fhall forbear this Confideration, it being as unneceffary to tell the Reader, that our *Play-Houfe* is in Fact the *Sink of Corruption and Debauchery;* that it is the general Rendezvous of the moft profligate Perfons of both Sexes; that it corrupts the Air, and turns the adjacent Places into publick Nufances; this is as unneceffary, as to tell him that the *Exchange* is a Place of *Merchandife.*

Now it is to be obferv'd, that this is not the State of the *Play-Houfe* through any accidental Abufe, as any innocent or good thing may be abufed; but that Corruption and Debauchery are the truly natural and genuine Effects of the *Stage-Entertainment.* Let not therefore any one fay, that he is not anfwerable for thofe Vices and Debaucheries which are occafion'd by the *Play-Houfe*; for fo far as he partakes of

C   the

the Pleafure of the *Stage*, and is an Encourager of it, fo far he is chargeable with thofe Diforders which neceffarily are occafion'd by it. If Evil arifes from our doing our Duty, or our Attendance at any *good Defign*, we are not to be frighted at it; but if Evil arifes from any thing as its *natural* and *genuine* Effect, in all fuch Cafes, fo far as we contribute to the Caufe, fo far we make our felves guilty of the Effects. So that all who any way affift the *Play-Houfe*, or ever encourage it by their Prefence, make themfelves chargeable, in fome degree, with all the Evils and Vices which follow from it. Since therefore it cannot be doubted by any one, whether the *Play-Houfe* be a Nurfery of Vice and Debauchery, fince the evil Effects it has upon People's Manners is as vifible as the Sun at Noon, one would imagine that all People of *Virtue* and *Modefty* fhould not only avoid it, but avoid it with the utmoft Abhorrence; that they fhould be fo far from entring into it, that they fhould deteft the very Sight of it. For what a Contradiction is it to common Senfe, to hear a Woman lamenting the miferable Lewdnefs and Debauchery of the Age, the vicious Tafte and irregular Pleafures of the World, and at the fame time dreffing herfelf to meet the lewdeft Part of the World at the Fountain-head of all Lewdnefs, and making herfelf one of that Crowd, where every abandon'd Wretch is glad to be prefent? She may fancy that fhe hates and abominates their Vices, but fhe may depend upon it, that till fhe hates and abominates the Place of vicious Pleafures; till fhe dare not come near an Entertainment, which is the Caufe of fo great Debauchery, and the Pleafure of the moft debauched People; till fhe is thus difpofed, fhe wants the trueft Sign of a real and religious Abhorrence of the Vices of the Age.

For, to wave all other Confiderations, I would only ask her a Queftion or two on the fingle Article of *Modefty*. What is Modefty? Is it a little *mechanical outfide* Behaviour, that goes no farther than a few *Forms* and *Modes* at particular Times and Places? Or is it a *real Temper*, a natural Difpofition of the Heart, that is founded in *Religion*? Now if Modefty is only a mechanical Obfervance of a little outfide Behaviour, then I can eafily perceive how a modeft Woman may frequent *Plays*; there is no Inconfiftency for fuch a one to be one thing in one Place, and another in another Place; to difdain an immodeft Converfation, and yet at the fame time, relifh and delight in immodeft and impudent Speeches in a publick *Play-Houfe*. But if Modefty is a *real Temper*

and

and Difpofition of the Heart, that is founded in the Principles of Religion, then I confefs I cannot comprehend, how a Perfon of fuch Modefty fhould ever come twice into the Play-Houfe. For if it is Reafon and Religion that has infpired her with a modeft Heart, that makes her careful of her Behaviour, that makes her hate and abhor every Word, or Look, or Hint in Converfation, that has the Appearance of Lewdnefs; that makes her fhun the Company of fuch as talk with too much Freedom: If fhe is thus modeft in *common Life*, from a Principle of Religion, a Temper of Heart, is it poffible for fuch a one (I don't fay to feek) but to bear with the Immodefty and Impudence of the *Stage*? For muft not Immodefty and Impudence, muft not loofe and wanton Difcourfe be the fame *hateful things*, and give the fame Offence to a modeft Mind, in one Place as in another? And muft not that Place, which is the Seat of Immodefty, where Men and Women are trained up in Lewdnefs; where almoft every Day in the Year is a Day devoted to the foolifh Reprefentations of *Rant*, *Luft*, and *Paffion*; muft not fuch a Place of all others be the moft odious to a Mind, that is *truly modeft* upon Principles of *Reafon* and *Religion*? One would fuppofe that fuch a Perfon fhould as much abominate the Place, as any other filthy Sight; and be as much offended with an Invitation to it, as if fhe was invited to fee an immodeft Picture. For the Reprefentations of the *Stage*, the inflamed Paffions of Lovers there defcrib'd, are as grofs an Offence to the Ear, as any Reprefentation that can offend the Eye.

It ought not to be concluded, that becaufe I affirm the *Play-Houfe* to be an Entertainment *contrary* to Modefty, that therefore I accufe all People as void of Modefty, who ever go to it. I might affirm, that *Tranfubftantiation* is contrary to all *Senfe* and *Reafon*; but then it would be a wrong Conclufion, to fay that I affirmed, that all who believe it are void of all *Senfe* and *Reafon*.

Now, as *Prejudices*, the Force of *Education*, the Authority of *Number*, the Way of the World, the Example of *great Names*, may make People *believe*; fo the fame Caufes may make People act againft *all Senfe and Reafon*, and be guilty of Practices, which no more fuit with the *Purity* of their Religion, than *Tranfubftantiation* agrees with *common Senfe*.

To proceed. *Trebonia* thus excufes her felf for going to the *Play-Houfe*. I go but feldom; and then either with my

Mother,

Mother, or my *Aunt*: We always know the Play before-hand, and never go on the *Sacrament*-Week: And what harm, pray, fays fhe, can there be in this? It breaks in upon no Rules of my Life. I neglect no Part of my Duty: I go to *Church*, and perform the fame Devotions at home, as on other Days.

It ought to be obferved, that this Excufe can only be al-low'd, where the Diverfion it felf is innocent: It muft there-fore firft be confider'd, what the Entertainment is in it felf; whether it be fuitable to the Spirit and Temper of Religion: For, if it is right and proper in it felf, it needs no Excufe; but if it be *wrong*, and *contrary* to Religion, we are not to ufe it *cautioufly*, but to avoid it *conftantly*.

Trebonia muft be told, that it is no Proof of the Innocency of a Thing, that it does not interfere with her *Hours of Du-ty*, nor break the Regularity of her Life; for, very wicked Ways of fpending Time, may yet be confiftent with a regu-lar Diftribution of our Hours. She muft therefore confider, not only whether fuch a Diverfion hinders the Regularity of her Life, or breaks in upon her Hours of Devotion, publick or private; but whether it hinders, or any way affects the *Spi-rit* and *Temper*, which all her Devotions afpire after. Is it conformable to that heavenly Affection, that Love of God, that Purity of Heart, that Wifdom of Mind, that Perfection of Holinefs, that Contempt of the World, that Watchfulnefs and Self-denial, that Humility and Fear of Sin, which Reli-gion requireth? Is it conformable to thefe Graces, which are to be the *daily Subject* of all her Prayers? This is the only way for her to know the *Innocency* of going to a Play. If what fhe there hears and fees, has no *Contrariety* to any *Grace* or *Virtue* that fhe prays for; if all that there paffes, be fit for the *Purity* and *Piety* of one that is led by the Spirit of Chrift, and is *working out* her *Salvation with fear and trembling*; if the Stage be an Entertainment, that may be thought to be according to the Will of God; then fhe difpofes of an Hour very innocently, tho' her *Mother* or her *Aunt* were not with her.

But if the *contrary* to all this be true; if moft of what fhe there *hears* and *fees*, be as contrary to the *Piety* and *Purity* of Chriftianity, as *Feafting* is contrary to *Fafting*; if the *Houfe* which fhe fupports with her *Money*, and encourages with her *Prefence*, be a notorious Means of Corruption, vifibly carry-ing on the Caufe of *Vice* and *Debauchery*; fhe muft not think her felf excus'd for being with her *Mother*.

Trebo-

Trebonia would perhaps think it ftrange, to hear one of her virtuous Acquaintance giving the like Reafon for going now and then to a *Mafquerade*.

Now, this Diverfion is new in our Country; and therefore moft People *yet* judge of it in the manner that they ought, becaufe they are not blinded by *Ufe and Cuftom*. But let any one give but the true Reafons, why a Perfon of Virtue and Piety fhould not go to *Mafquerades*; and the fame Reafons will as plainly fhew, that Perfons of Virtue and Piety fhould keep at as great a diftance from the *Play-Houfe*. For, the Entertainment of the *Stage* is more directly oppofite to the Purity of Religion, than *Mafquerades*; and is befides as certain a Means of Corruption, and ferves all bad Ends in as great a degree as they do. They only differ, as bad Things of the fame Kind may differ from one another. So that if the evil Ufe, and ill Confequences of *Mafquerades*, be a fufficient Reafon to deter People of Piety from partaking of them; the fame evil Ufe, and ill Confequences of the *Stage*, ought to keep all People of Virtue from it. If People will confult their *Tempers* only, they may take the Entertainment of one, and condemn the other; as following the fame Guide, they may abhor *Intemperance*, and indulge *Malice*: But if they will confult Religion, and make that the Ground of their Opinions, they will find more and ftronger Reafons for a *Conftant Abhorrence* of the *Stage*, than of *Mafquerades*.

Again: If *Trebonia* fhould hear a Perfon excufing her Ufe of *Paint*, in this manner; That truly fhe painted but *very feldom*; that fhe always faid her Prayers firft; that fhe never us'd it on *Sundays*, or the Week before the *Communion*: *Trebonia* would pity fuch a *Mixture* of Religion and Weaknefs. She would defire her to ufe her Reafon, and either to allow *Painting* to be innocent, fuitable to the *Sobriety* and *Humility* of a Chriftian, or elfe to think it as unlawful at one Time, as at another. But, *Trebonia*, would you not think it ftill ftranger, that fhe fhould condemn *Painting* as *odious* and *finful*, and yet think that the *Regularity* of her Life, and the *Exactnefs* of her Devotions, might make it lawful for her to paint *now and then*?

I don't doubt but you plainly fee the Weaknefs and Folly of fuch a Pretence for *Painting*, under fuch Rules, at certain Times. And if you would but as impartially confider your Pretences for going fometimes to the Play-Houfe, under the fame Rules, you would certainly find them more weak

and

and unreasonable. For *Painting* may with more Reason be reckoned an *innocent Ornament*, than the Play-House an *innocent Diversion*. And it supposes a greater *Vanity* of Mind, a more *perverted* Judgment, and a deeper Corruption of Heart, to seek the Diversion of the *Stage*, than to take the Pleasure of a *borrow'd Colour*. Painting, when consider'd in it self, is undoubtedly a great Sin; but when it is compared to the Use of the Stage, it is but as the *Mote* compared to the *Beam*.

I know you are offended at this *Comparison*, because you judge by your *Temper* and *Prejudices*, and don't consider the things as they are in themselves, by the pure Light of *Reason* and *Religion*. *Painting* has not been the way of your Family; it is suppos'd to be the Practice but of *very few*; and those who use it, endeavour to *conceal* it: this makes you readily condemn it. On the contrary, your *Mother* and your *Aunt* carry you to the *Play*; you see *virtuous* People there, and the same Persons that fill our *Churches*; so that your *Temper* is as much engaged to think it lawful to go sometimes to a *Play*, as it is engaged to think the Use of *Paint* always odious and sinful.

Lay aside therefore these Prejudices for a while, and fancy that you had been trained up in some Corner of the World in the Principles of Christianity, and had never heard either of the *Play-House* or *Painting*. Imagine now that you was to examine the Lawfulness of them by the Doctrines of Scripture; you would first desire to be told the Nature of these things, and what they meant. You would be told, that *Painting* was the borrowing of *Colours* from Art, to make the Face look more beautiful. Now tho' you found no express Text of Scripture against *Painting*, you would find that it was expressly against Tempers required in Scripture; you would therefore condemn it, as proceeding from a Vanity of Mind, and Fondness of Beauty. You would see that the Harm of Painting consisted in this, that it proceeded from a Temper of Mind contrary to the Sobriety and Humility of a Christian; which indeed is harm enough; because this Humility and Sobriety of Mind is as essential to Religion, as Charity and Devotion. So that in judging according to Scripture, you would hold it as unreasonable to *paint sometimes*, as to be sometimes *malicious, indevout, proud,* or *false*.

You are now to consider the *Stage*; you are to keep close to Scripture, and fancy that you yet know nothing of *Plays*. You ask therefore first, what the *Stage* or *Play-House* is? You

are

are told that it is a *Place* where all forts of People meet to be entertain'd with *Difcourfes, Aĉtions,* and *Reprefentations*; which are recommended to the Heart by beautiful Scenes, the Splendor of Lights, and the Harmony of Mufick. You are told that thefe Difcourfes are the Inventicn of Men of Wit and Imagination, which defcribe imaginary *Intrigues* and *Scenes* of *Love,* and introduce *Men* and *Women* difcourfing, raving, and aĉting in all the wild, indecent Tranfports of *Luft* and *Paffion.* You are told, that the Diverfion partly confifts of *lewd* and *prophane* Songs fung to fine Mufick, and partly of extravagant Dialogues between *immodeft Perfons* talking in a Stile of *Love* and *Madnefs,* that is no where elfe to be found, and entertaining the *Chriftian Audience* with all the Violence of Paffion, Corruption of Heart, Wantonnefs of Mind, Immodefty of Thought, and prophane Jefts, that the Wit of the *Poet* is able to invent. You are told, that the *Players,* Men and Women, are trained up to aĉt and re-prefent all the Defcriptions of Luft and Paffion in the *livelieft manner,* to add a Lewdnefs of Aĉtion to lewd Speeches; that they get their Livelihood by *Curfing, Swearing,* and *Ranting* for three Hours together to an Affembly of *Chri-ftians.*

Now though you find no particular Text of Scripture con-demning the *Stage,* or *Tragedy* or *Comedy,* in exprefs Words; yet what is much more, you find that fuch Entertainments are a grofs Contradiĉtion to the *whole Nature* of Religion; they are not contrary to this or that particular Temper, but are contrary to that *whole Turn of Heart* and *Mind* which Religion requires. Painting is contrary to *Humility,* and therefore is to be avoided as finful, but the Entertainment of the *Stage,* as it confifts of *blafphemous* Expreffions, *wicked* Speeches, *fwearing, curfing,* and *prophaning* the Name of God, as it abounds with *impious* Rant, *filthy* Jefts, *diftraĉted* Paffions, grofs Defcriptions of *Luft,* and *wanton Songs,* is a *Contradiĉtion to every Doĉtrine* that our Saviour and his Apo-ftles have taught us. So that to abhor *Painting* at all times, becaufe it fuppofes a Vanity of Mind, and is contrary to Humility, and yet think there is a lawful Time to go to the *Play-Houfe,* is as contrary to common Senfe, as if a Man fhould hold that it was lawful fometimes to offend againft *all the Doĉtrines* of Religion, and yet always unlawful to offend againft *any one* Doĉtrine of Religion.

If therefore you was to come (as I fuppofed) from fome Corner of the World, where you had been ufed to live and

judge

judge by the Rules of Religion; and upon your Arrival here, had been told, what Painting and the *Stage* was; as you would not expect to fee Persons of *religious Humility* carrying their Daughters to *Paint-Shops*, or inviting their pious Friends to go along with them; fo much lefs would you expect to hear, that *devout*, *pious* and *modeft* Women carried their Daughters, and invited their virtuous Friends to meet them at the Play. Leaft of all could you imagine, that there were any People too *pious* and *devout*, to indulge the Vanity of *Painting*; and yet not devout and pious enough, to abhor the Immodefty, Prophanenefs, Ribaldry, Immorality, and Blafphemy of the *Stage*.

To proceed. A *polite Writer* (a) of a late Paper thought he had fufficiently ridiculed a certain Lady's Pretenfions to *Piety*; when, fpeaking of her *Clofet*, he fays,

> *Together l.e her Prayer-Book and Paint,*
> *At once t'improve the Sinner and the Saint.*

Now, whence comes it that this Writer judges fo rightly, and fpeaks the Truth fo plainly, in the Matter of Painting? Whence comes it, that the Generality of his Readers think his Obfervation juft, and join with him in it? It is becaufe Painting is not yet an *acknowledg'd Practice*, but is for the moft part reckon'd a *fhameful Inftance* of Vanity. Now, as we are not prejudiced in Favour of this Practice, and have no Excufes to make for our *own Share* in it, fo we judge of it impartially, and immediately perceive its Contrariety to a Religious *Temper* and *State* of Mind. This *Writer* faw this in fo ftrong a Light, that he does not fcruple to fuppofe, that *Paint* is as natural and proper a Means to improve the *Sinner*, as the Prayer-Book is to improve the Saint.

I fhould therefore hope, that it need not be imputed to any *Sowrenefs* of Temper, Religious *Weaknefs*, or *Dulnefs* of Spirits, if a *Clergyman* fhould imagine, that the *Prophanenefs*, *Debauchery*, *Lewdnefs*, and *Blafphemy* of the *Stage*, is as natural a Means to improve the *Sinner*, as a *Bottle of Paint*: or if he fhould venture to fhew, that the *Church* and the *Play-Houfe* are as ridiculous a Contradiction, and do no more fuit with the *fame* Perfon, than the *Prayer-Book and Paint*.

(a) *Spectat.* N°. 79.

I fhall

I shall now make a Reflexion or two upon the present celebrated Entertainment of the *Stage*, which is so much to the Taste of this Christian Country, that it has been acted almost every Night this whole Season, I mean *Apollo* and *Daphne*.

The first Scene is said to be, a *magnificent Palace discover'd: Venus attended with Graces and Pleasures.*

Now how is it possible, that such a Scene as this should be fit for the Entertainment of Christians? Can *Venus* and her *Graces* and *Pleasures* talk any Language that is *like* themselves, but what must be *unlike* to the Spirit of Christianity? The very proposing such a Scene as this, supposes the Audience to be fit for the Entertainment of *Lust* and *Wantonness.* For what else can *Venus* and her *Pleasures* offer to them? Had we any thing of the Spirit of Christianity in us, or were earnestly desirous of those holy Tempers, which are to render us pure in the Eyes of God, we should abominate the very Proposal of such a Scene as this, as knowing that it must be an Entertainment fitter for *publick Stews*, than for People who make any Pretences to the Holiness and Purity of the Spirit of Christ. The Scripture saith, *Mortify therefore your members which are upon earth, fornication, uncleanness, inordinate affection, evil concupiscence.* This is the Religion by which we are to be saved. But can the Wit of Man invent any thing more contrary to this, than an Entertainment from *Venus* attended with her *Pleasures?* That People should have such a Religion as this, and at the same time such an Entertainment, is an astonishing Instance of the Degeneracy of the present State of Christianity amongst us. For if the first Scene had been the *Devil attended with Fiends, cursing and blaspheming,* no one could shew that such a Scene was more contrary to the Religion of *Christians,* than a Scene with *Venus* and her *Pleasures.* And if the Devil himself had been consulted by our *Stage-Wits,* which of these Scenes he had rather have, he would certainly have chosen *Venus* and her *Pleasures,* as much fitter to debauch and corrupt a Christian Audience, than a Scene of *cursing* and *blaspheming.*

The Scripture thus describeth the Infatuation of the old Idolaters. *And none considereth in his heart, neither is there knowledge, nor understanding to say, I have burnt part of it in the fire; yea, I have also baked bread upon the coals thereof, and shall I make the residue thereof an abomination? Shall*

I fall

I fall down to the Stock of a tree? * It is here reckon'd a
ſtrange Inſtance of their Blindneſs, that they did not make ſo
eaſy a Reflexion upon the nature of things. But how near
are we to this Blindneſs, if we don't make as eaſy a Reflexion
upon this Entertainment; for the very mentioning of ſuch a
Scene as this, is as plain a Demonſtration, that the Entertainment is contrary to our Religion, as the *burning* of Wood,
and its falling into *Aſhes*, is a Demonſtration that Wood is
of a Nature contrary to God. How are we therefore more
enlighten'd, if none of us conſidereth in his Heart, neither is
there Knowledge, nor Underſtanding in us to ſay, *Theſe are
the filthy Deities of the Devil's Invention, with which he pol-
luted and defiled the Heathen World; and ſhall we ſtill preſerve
their Power amongſt us? Shall we make ſuch Abominations our
Diverſion?*

For if we worſhip the God of *Purity*, if we cannot worſhip him but with Hearts devoted to Purity, what have we
to do with theſe Images of Lewdneſs? If we dreſs a *Venus*,
and celebrate her Power, and make her *Graces* and *Pleaſures*
meet us in wanton *Forms*, and wanton *Language*; is it not as
abſurd, as contrary to our Religion, as to ſet up a *Baal*, in
the Temple of God? What greater Contradiction is there,
either to Reaſon or Religion, in one Caſe than in the other?
Baal is as fit for our Devotions, as *Venus* is for our Rejoycings
and Praiſes.

So that the very naming of ſuch a Scene as this is *unlawful Language*, and carries as great a Contrariety to our Religion, as the Worſhip of *Baal*.

Here two Women. (whom I ſuppoſe to be baptiz'd Chriſtians) repreſent *Venus* and *Diana* in this Language.

> Ven. *Am'rous Kiſſes*,
> Dian. *Nuptial Bliſſes*,
> { *Lovers Pleaſures*,
> { Cupid's *Treaſures*,
> { *Are the Sweets that Life improve.*

Now if a common *Proſtitute* was to come drunk out of a
Brandy Shop ſinging theſe Words, ſhe would act like herſelf.
No one could ſay that ſhe had forgot her Character, or was
ſinging one way, and *living* another. And I dare ſay, there

---

* *Iſa.* xliv. 19.

is no *Rake* in the Audience so debauch'd, as not to think this a sufficient Celebration of the Praises and Happiness of his Pleasures.

But what do other People do here? Is there any Entertainment in this Place for *pious*, *sober*, and *devout* Minds? Does it become them to sing the Praises of Debauchery, or sit amongst those that do?

When we hear of a *Witches Feast*, we don't hear of any but *Witches* that go to it: The Mirth and Joy of such Meetings is left wholly to themselves. Now if these impudent Celebrations of *Venus* and her *Pleasures* were left wholly to *Rakes* and *Prostitutes*; if we reckon'd it an Entertainment as contrary to Religion, as a *Witches Feast*; it would only shew, that we judged as rightly in one Case, as in the other. And indeed, one would think, that no Christian need be told, that *Venus* and her *Graces* are as much the Devil's *Machinery*, as *Witches* and *Imps*.

To proceed.

If a Person in Conversation was to addreſs himself to a *Modeſt* Lady in these words; *Am'rous Kiſſes*, &c. she would think her self very ill us'd; and that she ought to resent such Treatment. She would think, that her *Modeſty* might well be question'd, if she bore such Language.

But how it is consistent with such Modesty, to hire People to entertain her with the same Language in Publick, is a Difficulty not easily to be explain'd. Can *Fathers* and *Mothers*, who sit here with their Children, recommend Purity to them at home, when they have carry'd them to hear the Praises of Lewdness, as the *Sweets which Life improve?*

If a Person was to make a publick Harangue in favour of *Image-Worſhip*, telling us, that it was the fineſt Means of raising the Heart to a Delight in God; we should think him a *very wicked* Man, and that the Ears and Hearts of Christians ought to deteſt such Discourses. Yet Christian People can meet in Crowds, and give their Money to have this repeated in their Ears, that *Am'rous Kiſſes, Lovers Pleaſures,* Cupid's *Treaſures, are the Sweets which Life improve.* This, it seems, is no *Idolatry.*

We are told in Scripture, that *Covetouſneſs is Idolatry*; and the Reason is, becauſe it alienates the Heart from God, and makes it reſt in something elſe. The covetous Man is an *Idolater*, becauſe his Heart says, that *Gain* and *Bags* of Gold are the *Sweets which Life improve.* And can we think that

that

that corrupt Heart, that celebrates *Luſt* and *Wantonneſs*, as
the *Sweets which Life improve*, is guilty of *leſs Idolatry*, than
he that ſays the ſame thing of Riches? As ſure as there is ſuch
a Sin as *Idolatry*, as ſure as the Sordid *Miſer* is guilty of it,
ſo ſure is it that theſe words are chargeable, not only with ex-
ceſſive *Immodeſty*, but plain *Idolatry*. For how do we think
that the *Pagans* worſhipp'd *Venus*? We cannot ſuppoſe that it
was with *Faſting* and *Prayer*, or any *ſerious* Devotions. No;
they paid her ſuch a Devotion, as the *Stage* now does; they
call'd upon her in *lewd* Songs, and prais'd her, in praiſing the
Pleaſures of Luſt and Impurity, in rejoicing in her mighty
Power, and celebrating her Pleaſures, as the true *Sweets which
Life improve*.

Theſe Women go on thus.

Dian.   *Still to languiſh*
Ven.   *With ſweet Anguiſh,*
　　　{ *Softly ſighing,*
　　　{ *Murm'ring, dying,*
　　　{ *Are th' immortal Gifts of Love.*

Here Muſick and Voices, as wanton as the Words, are
employ'd to make a deeper Impreſſion on the Hearts of the
Audience. Here enter *Bacchus*, *Pan*, and *Silenus*, attended
with *Satyrs*, *Fawns* and *Sylvans*.

And indeed, they enter very properly; for the Diſcourſe is
very agreeable to their Nature. But what have Chriſtians to
do with this Company? Do they come here to *renounce* their
Religion? Or can they think that this Society, with the moſt
beaſtly *Images* that the Heathen World could invent, is
a Society that they may partake of, without *Renouncing*
Chriſt?

Our Religion chargeth us, not to *keep company, if any one
that is called a Brother, be a fornicator,* * &c. But where
have we left our Religion, if we not only company with People devoted to Impurity, but make their Company our Delight, and *hire* them to entertain us with all the lewd Imaginations that can be invented? If we are not content with
this, but *conjure* up all the impure *Fictions* of the Heathen

* 1 Cor. 5. 11.

World,

World, and make their *imaginary Deities* more vile and wanton than ever they made them, to render them agreeable to our Chriſtian Minds ; ſhall we reckon this amongſt our *ſmall Sins* ? Shall we think it a pardonable Infirmity, to partake of ſuch an Entertainment as this?

The Apoſtle ſaith, *Ye cannot drink the Cup of the Lord, and the Cup of Devils : Ye cannot be partakers of the Lord's Table, and the Table of Devils* *. And can we think that we are not drinking the Cup of Devils, or that we are not at the Devil's Table, when his moſt favourite Inſtruments of Impiety, *Venus, Bacchus, Silenus, Satyrs* and *Fauns*, are the Company that we meet to be entertain'd with ? If this is not being at the Devil's Table, he had no Table in the Heathen World. For ſurely, they who call up Devils to their Entertainment, who cannot be enough delighted, unleſs the impious Dæmons of the Heathen World converſe with them, are in a ſtricter Communication with the Devil, than they who only eat of that Meat which had been offer'd in Sacrifice.

Our bleſſed Saviour ſaith, *He that looketh upon a woman, to luſt after her, hath already committed adultery with her in his heart.* Can we reckon our ſelves his Diſciples, who hire our Fellow-Chriſtians, and Chriſtian Women, (whoſe chief Ornament is a ſincere Modeſty) to ſing in merry Aſſemblies ſuch Words as theſe : *Still to languiſh, with ſweet Anguiſh ; Softly ſighing, murm'ring, dying, Are th' immortal Gifts of Love ?*

Who can ſay that I carry Matters too high, when I call this, *renouncing* Chriſtianity ? For, can any Words be more expreſsly contrary to the Doctrine of our Saviour, and that in ſo important a Point ? And does not he ſufficiently renounce Chriſtianity, who renounces ſo great a Doctrine, that has Chriſt for its Author ?

If we were to make a Jeſt of the *Sacraments* in our merry Aſſemblies, we ſhould ſhew as much Regard to Chriſtianity, as by ſuch Diſcourſes as theſe. For all *lewd Diſcourſes* are as plainly contrary to eſſential Doctrines of Scripture, as any Ridicule upon the Sacraments that can be invented. It may be you could not ſit in the *Play-Houſe*, if you ſaw *Baptiſm* made a Jeſt of, and its Uſe reproach'd. But pray, why

---

* 1 Cor. 10. 21.

don't

don't you think that there is as much *Prophaneneſs* and *Ir-religion* in impudent Speeches and Songs? Has not Chriſt ſaid as much about *Purity* of Heart, as about either of the *Sacraments*? Has not he made Chaſtity of Heart as neceſſary to Salvation, as the Sacraments? How comes it then, that an impudent Praiſe of Luſt and Wantonneſs is not as *prophane*, as a Ridicule upon the Sacraments? What Rule of Reaſon or Religion do you go by, when you think it highly ſinful to ſit and hear the *Sacraments* jeſted upon, and yet are chearful and delighted with ſuch Songs and Diſcourſes, as ridicule *Chaſtity* of Heart, and religious *Modeſty*? Can you ſuppoſe, that in the Eyes of God you appear as a better Chriſtian, than thoſe who make merry with prophaning the Sacraments? If you can think this, you muſt hold that the Sacraments are more eſſential to Religion than *Purity* of Heart; and that it is more acceptable to God to *waſh*, than to be *clean*; more pleaſing to him to treat the *Altar* as holy, than to live in *Holineſs* of Heart.

The Sacraments have nothing valuable in their own Nature; they are only uſeful to Chriſtians, and to be treated with Reverence, becauſe Chriſt has appointed them as Means. of Holineſs. But Purity and Chaſtity of Heart is an eſſential and internal Excellence, that by its own Nature perfects the Soul, and renders it more acceptable to God. To abhor therefore a Jeſt upon the *Sacraments*, and yet divert our ſelves with *impure* Rant, and *lewd* Songs, is being like thoſe who *abhor Idols*, and yet *commit Sacrilege*.

All therefore who partake of this ſinful Entertainment, who take their Share of Mirth in ſuch Scenes of Impurity and Lewdneſs, muſt look upon themſelves not only as Offenders againſt the Laws of *Purity*, but alſo as chargeable with ſuch *Irreligion* and *Prophaneneſs*, as they are, who are merry in ſuch Meetings as ridicule and banter the Uſe of the Holy Sacraments.

It is a great Aggravation of the Guilt of theſe Aſſemblies, that Women are employ'd to lay aſide the peculiar Ornament of their Sex, and to add an Immodeſty of Action and Addreſs to immodeſt Speeches. If we knew of an Aſſembly, where Clergymen met to ridicule the *ſacred Rites* of Religion for the ſake of entertaining the Audience with *Eloquence*; if we ſhould find that great Part of the Audience were *Clergymen*, who could not forbear an Entertainment ſo contrary to their Profeſſion, it would eaſily be ſeen, that ſuch a ſinful

I

Enter-

Entertainment was more unreasonable, becaufe Clergymen acted in it, and Clergymen came to be entertain'd with it.

Now this is the Cafe of the Stage-Entertainment; Women are as particularly called to a *fingular Modefty*, as Clergymen are to the Duties of their Profeffion; if therefore Women act Parts in lewd and impudent Entertainments, they have as much forgot themfelves, and appear as *deteftable*, as Clergymen that talk *prophanely*. And if other Women come to delight themfelves with feeing their *Sifters* acting fo contrary to themfelves, and the peculiar Duties of their Condition, they as much forget themfelves, as thofe *Clergy* who fhould meet to fee their *Brethren* raife Diverfion out of *Prophanenefs*. When therefore virtuous and prudent Women think they may go to the *Stage*, where Women fo openly depart from the Decencies which are neceffary to their Sex, let them confider what they would think of fuch virtuous and prudent Divines, as fhould meet to fee Clergymen openly contradict the Duties of their facred Office. For it is the fame Abfurdity, for modeft Women to take pleafure in a Diverfion, where Women are *immodeft*, as for a good Clergyman to be pleas'd with a Meeting, where Clergymen are *prophane*. This muft be own'd to be ftrictly true, unlefs it can be fhewn, that *Impudence* and *Immodefty* are not fo contrary to the Duties of *Women*, as *Prophanenefs* is contrary to the Duty of a *Clergyman*. For if there is the fame Contrariety, then it muft be equally monftrous for Women to encourage a Number of Women in an immodeft Way of Life, as for *Bifhops* and *Priefts* to encourage a Number of Clergymen in a State of *Prophanenefs*.

Let us now take one Step farther in this Entertainment. The *Stage* has now upon it, *Venus, Bacchus, Silenus, Pan, Satyrs, Fawns, Sylvans, Bacchanals,* and *Bacchantes.* Now if there were really fuch Beings as thefe, one would not wonder to fee them got together. As they have all one common Nature of *Vilenefs,* they are fufficiently recommended to one another. But is it not aftonifhing, that thefe *fictitious Beings,* which are only imaginary Reprefentations of fuch *Luft, Senfuality* and *Madnefs,* as never had any real Exiftence, but were invented by the Devil for the Delufion of the Heathen World, fhould be preferv'd to talk their filthy Language to Congregations of *Chriftians!* And perhaps *Silenus* never fo publickly recommended *Luft* and *Impudence* in any Heathen Affembly, as he does here amongft Chriftians. For our

Stage

Stage has made him a fine Singer, that his Lewdness may have all the Recommendation, which a merry, strong Voice can give it.

Silenus. *Tho' envious old Age seems in part to impair me;*
And make me the Sport of the Wanton and Gay;
Brisk Wine shall recruit, as Life's Winter shall wear me;
And I still have a Heart to do what I may.
Then, Venus, *bestow me some Dam'sel of Beauty;*
Here's Bacchus *will furnish the cherishing Glass;*
Silenus, *tho' grey, shall to both do his Duty;*
And now clasp the Bottle, and then clasp the Lass.

Surely no one will now think that I carry'd the Charge too high, when I call'd the *Play-House* the House of the *Devil;* for if his *fictitious Beings,* talking his Language, and acting such Parts as these, be not a sufficient Proof that it is his Work that is here carrying on, it is in vain to pretend to prove any thing: There is no Certainty that two and two are four.

If our Eyes could shew us the *holy Angels* in our Church-Assemblies, it would not be a stronger Proof of the Divine Presence, than the seeing such Images as these, and the hearing such Language from them, is a Proof that the *Stage* is the Devil's Ground. For how can he more certainly assure us of his Presence in any Place, than by *Satyrs, Bacchanals, Bacchantes,* and such like Images of Lewdness? He cannot appear to us as a Spirit; he must therefore get such *Beings as these* to appear for him; or, what seems to be more to his Purpose, make deluded Christians supply their Places. If therefore there be any certain Marks of the Devil's Power or Presence in any Assemblies, Places, or Temples of the Heathen World, the same are as certain Marks of his Power and Presence in our *Play-House.*

Again; Is it any Argument that the *Church* is God's House, because we there meet the *Ministers* of God, who act in his Name; because we there sing divine Hymns, hear holy Instructions, and raise our Hearts unto God and heavenly Matters; is this any Proof that we are then drawn near to God? If therefore there be a Place set apart for *lewd* and *prophane* Discourses, where the same Beings are introduc'd as filled Heathen Temples, where we celebrate their Power, and praise their Being with wanton Songs and impure Rant, and where we open our Hearts to the Impressions of wild and
dis-

diſorder'd Paſſions, is not this as certain a Proof, that ſuch a *Place* muſt belong to ſome Being that is *contrary* to God, and that we are then as certainly drawn near to him? He* that does not ſee this with a ſufficient Clearneſs, could never have ſeen that the Devil had any Power or Worſhip in the Heathen World. You muſt therefore obſerve, that the *Play-Houſe* is not call'd the Houſe of the Devil only by way of Terror; and to fright you from a bad Place; but it is called ſo, becauſe it really is ſo in the ſtricteſt, fulleſt Senſe of the Words.

Let us now ſuppoſe, that the Diſorders of the Stage cannot drive you from it; and that you are no more offended at the Meeting of theſe filthy Dæmons of the Heathen World, than if you was to meet your Friends.

If this be your Caſe, how will you prove that your Religion has had any Effect upon you? Or that it has done you the leaſt good? For if the ſame Lewdneſs and Immorality plea-ſes you, which pleaſed the Worſhippers of *Venus*; if you de-light in ſuch *Rant* and *Madneſs*, as was the Delight of *Bac-chanals* and *Bacchantes*, is not this a Proof that you have rhe ſame *Heart* and *Temper* that they had? And if you are like Idolaters in that which conſtituted their Idolatry, have you any Reaſon to think that Chriſtianity has had any Effect upon you? It would even be *Prophaneneſs* in any one to pre-tend to the true Spirit of Chriſtianity, ſo long as he can take pleaſure in ſuch an Entertainment as this. For what is there that is unlike to the Spirit of Chriſt, if this is not? Who that can rejoyce in the Lewdneſs and Beſtiality of a *Silenus*, and the impure Rant of vile Dæmons, can make any Pretences to a reaſonable Piety? Does this Company look as if we had any thing holy and divine in our Tempers? Is this living in the Spirit of Chriſt? Is this the way to be as the Angels of God when we dye? Shall we go from the Pleaſures of *Bac-chus, Silenus, Bacchanals* and *Bacchantes*, to the Choir of bleſ-ſed Spirits that are above? Is there any Reaſonableneſs or Fitneſs in theſe things? Why ſhould we think, that ſuch a Life as this will have an End ſo contrary to it?

We reckon it ſtrange Groſsneſs of Mind in the *Turks*, to expect a *Paradiſe* of carnal Delights. But what a Degree of Groſsneſs is it in us, to know the God of Purity, and hope for a Heaven which only the *pure in Heart* ſhall enjoy, and yet call up all the vile *Fictions* of Luſt and Senſuality, that corrupted the Heathen World, to entertain our Hearts? That from their Mouths we may hear the Praiſes of Debauchery

E   and

and Wantonnefs? Let any one but confider this, as every thing ought to be confidered, by the pure Light of Reafon and Religion, and he will find that the Ufe of the Stage may be reckon'd amongft our worft Sins, and that it is as great a Contradiction to our Religion, as any Corruption or vile Practice of the Heathen World.

I have made thefe few Reflexions upon this Entertainment, not becaufe it exceeds the ordinary Wickednefs of the Stage, but for the contrary Reafon, becaufe it is far fhort of it, and is much lefs offenfive than moft of our *Plays*. That by fhewing the *Stage* to be fo impious and deteftable, fo contradictory to all Chriftian Piety, in an Entertainment that is moderate, if compared with almoft all our Plays, there might be no room left for fober Chriftians to be at any Peace with it. They who would fee how much the Impieties of the Stage exceed what I have here obferv'd of this Entertainment, may confult Mr. *Collier's* fhort View of the Stage, Sir *Richard Blackmore's* Eſſays, and a *ferious Remonſtrance*, &c. by Mr. *Bedford*.

To return : *Levis* hears all thefe Arguments againft the *Stage*; he owns they are very plain, and ftrictly prove all that they pretend to; he does not offer one word againft them, but ftill *Levis* has an Anfwer for them *all*, without anfwering any *one* of them. I have, fays he, my own Experience, that thefe Diverfions never did me any hurt, and therefore I fhall ufe them.

But *Levis* does not confider, that this very Anfwer fhews, that he is very much hurt by them; that they have fo much diforder'd his Underftanding, that he will defend his Ufe of them in the moft abfurd manner imaginable, rather than be driven from them by any Arguments from Religion. For how can a Man fhew that he is more hurt by any Practice, or that it has more blinded and perverted his Mind, than by appealing to his own inward Experience in Defenfe of it, againft the plain Nature and Reafon of things? Let *Levis* look at this way of reafoning in other Matters. If a Perfon that prays in an *unknown Tongue*, fhould difregard all the Arguments that are brought to fhew the Abfurdity of it, and reft contented with faying, that it never hurt his Devotion, but that he was as much affected in that way, as he could poffibly be in any other : *Levis* would certainly tell fuch a one, that he had loft his Underftanding ; and that his long

Ufe

Ufe of fuch abfurd Devotions, made him talk fo abfurdly about them.

Again. If a Worfhipper of *Images* was, in Anfwer to the Second Commandment, only to fay, that he had his own Experience that he found no hurt by them; and that he had the fame Devotion of Heart to God, as if he did not worfhip *Images*. Or, fuppofe another Perfon to keep very ill Company; and when he is told, that *evil communications corrupt good manners*, fhould content himfelf with faying, that he would ftill ufe the fame ill Company, becaufe he was fure it did him no hurt, nor made any Impreffion upon him. Now as *Levis* would be fure that a Man was notorioufly hurt by the Worfhip of *Images*, that fhould thus blindly defend them, and that the other is fufficiently hurt by ill Company, who fhould fo obftinately ftick to it; fo he ought to be as fure, that he himfelf is fufficiently hurt either by Plays, or fomething elfe, when with an equal Blindnefs he defends his Ufe of them.

Farther: When *Levis* fays, that he is fure that the Ufe of Plays does him no harm; let him confider, what he means by that Speech. Does he mean, that tho' he ufes the Diverfion of the Stage, yet he finds himfelf in the true State of Religion; that he has all thofe holy Tempers in that degree of Perfection which Chriftianity requireth? Now, if he cannot fay this; how can he fay, he is fure that Plays do him no harm? If a Perfon was to affirm, that Intemperance did him no hurt; it would be expected, that he fhould own that he was in a perfect State of Health: For, if he had any Diforder, or ill Habit of Body, he could not fay, that his Intemperance did not contribute towards it. In like manner, if *Levis* will maintain, that Plays do no ways diforder him, or corrupt his Heart; he muft affirm, that he has no Diforder or Corruption of Heart belonging to him; for if he has, he cannot fay, that his Ufe of Plays does not contribute towards it.

When therefore *Levis* fays, Plays do me no harm at all; it is the fame thing as if he had faid, I have no Diforder at all upon me; My Heart, and all my Tempers, are in that exact State of Purity and Perfection that they fhould be.

Again. Let *Levis* confider, that his Tafte and Relifh of the Stage, is a Demonftration that he is already hurt by fomething or other; and that his Heart is not in a right State of Religion. *Levis* thinks this is a very cenforious Accufation; becaufe he is known to be a very good Churchman, to live

a regua regular Life for the moſt part, to be charitable, and a Well-wiſher to all good Deſigns. All this is true of *Levis* : But then it is as ſtrictly true, that his Taſte for Plays is a Demonſtration, that his Heart is not in a right State of Religion. For, does *Levis* think, that his frequenting the Church is any Sign of the State of his Heart ? Am I to believe, that he has inward Diſpoſitions, that ſuit with the holy Strains of Divine Service, becauſe he likes to be at Church ? I grant, I am to believe this ; there is good Reaſon for it. But then, if *Levis* uſes the *Play-Houſe*, if the diſorder'd Paſſions, the lewd Images, the profane Rant, and immodeſt Parts that are there acted, are a Pleaſure to him ; is not this as ſtrong a Demonſtration, that he has ſome Diſpoſitions and Tempers, that ſuit with theſe Diſorders ? If I am to conclude any thing from a Man's liking and frequenting Divine Service ; is there not as certain a Concluſion to be drawn from a Man's liking and uſing the Stage ? For the Stage can no more be lik'd, without having ſome inward Corruptions that are ſuitable to the Diſorders that are there repreſented, than the Divine Service can be a Pleaſure to any one, that has no Holineſs or Devotion in his Heart.

It is infallibly certain, that all Pleaſures ſhew the *State* and *Condition* of our Minds ; and that nothing can pleaſe us, but what ſuits with ſome Diſpoſitions and Tempers that are within us ; ſo that when we ſee a Man's Pleaſures, we are ſure that we ſee a great deal of his Nature. All *Forms* of Life, all *outward* Actions may deceive us. We can't abſolutely ſay, that People have ſuch Tempers, becauſe they do ſuch Actions ; but where-ever People place any *Delight*, or receive any *Pleaſures*, there we have an infallible Token of ſomething in their Nature, and of what Tempers they have within them.

Diverſions therefore, and Pleaſures, which are reckon'd ſuch uncertain Means of judging of the *State* of Men's Minds, are of all Means the moſt certain ; becauſe nothing can pleaſe us, or affect us, but what is according to our Nature, and finds ſomething within us that is ſuitable to it. Had we not inward Diſpoſitions of *Tenderneſs* and *Compaſſion*, we ſhould not find our ſelves ſoften'd and mov'd with *miſerable* Objects. Had we not ſomething *harmonious* in our Nature, we ſhould not find our ſelves pleas'd with Strains of *Muſick*. In like manner, had we not in our Nature lively Seeds of all thoſe Diſorders which are acted upon the Stage, were there not ſome
inward

inward Corruption, that finds it felf gratify'd by all the irregu-
lar Paffions *that are there reprefented*, we fhould find no more
Pleafure in the Stage, than blind Men find in *Pictures*, or deaf
Men in *Mufick*.

And, on the other fide, if we were full of the contrary
Tempers, were our Hearts full of Affections contrary to thofe
on the *Stage*, were we deeply affected with defires of Purity
and Holinefs ; we fhould find our felves as much offended
with all that paffes upon the Stage, as *mild* and *gentle* Natures
are offended at the fight of *Cruelty* and *Barbarity*. Thefe
Things are of the utmoft Certainty.

All People therefore who ufe the *Stage*, have as much Affurance that their Heart is not in a right State of Religion, as
they poffibly can have of any Thing that relates to themfelves.

I hope, none of my Readers will think this too general,
or too rafh an Affertion ; but that they will rather obferve,
that it is founded on fuch Evidence of Reafon, as cannot be
rejected, without rejecting every Thing that is plain and certain in Human Nature. They muft not think it a fufficient
Anfwer to this, to confider either how good they are themfelves, or how many excellent Perfons they know, who do
not abftain from the Stage : For this is a way of reafoning,
that is not allow'd in any other Cafe.

Now, when it is affirm'd that all Perfons who are pleas'd
with the *Stage*, muft have fome Corruptions of Heart, that
are gratify'd with the corrupt Paffions which are there acted ;
is not this as plain and evident, as if it were faid, that all
who are pleas'd with feeing barbarous Actions, muft have
fome Seeds of Barbarity in their Nature? If you are delighted with the Stroke of the *Whip*, and love to fee the *Blood*
fly ; is it not paft all doubt, that you have a Barbarity within
you? And if *impure* Speeches, if *wanton* Amours, if *wild*
Paffions, and *immoral* Rant, can give you any Delight ; is it
not equally paft all doubt, that you have fomething of all
thefe Diforders in your Nature ? Is it any more uncharitable
to affirm this, than to affirm, that all who love to fee the
Blood fly, have fomething barbarous in their Nature ? Is there
any more Rafhnefs or Severity in it, than in faying, that all
who love fuch or fuch Strains of *Mufick*, have fome Difpofition in their Nature, that is gratified by them ?

It fignifies nothing therefore to fay, that you know fuch or
fuch excellent Perfons who are pleas'd with the *Stage*, whom
no one ought to fufpect to be defective in Piety ; it is as ab-

2

furd

furd as to fay, that you know excellent Perfons who are
pleas'd with feeing barbarous Actions, whom no one ought
to fufpect to be defective in *Tendernefs*. If you delight in
barbarous Sights, and are pleas'd with the Groans and Pains
of the Afflicted, I don't *fufpect* you to be defective in *Tendernefs*, you have put your Cafe out of all Sufpicion, you have
prov'd that you have a Barbarity in your Nature. So that if
you delight in the *Stage*, if you tafte and relifh its Entertainment, I don't *fufpect* you to be *defective* in Piety; you have
put your Cafe beyond Sufpicion; you have prov'd that you
have Difpofitions in your Nature, that are gratify'd by the
diforderly Paffions of the *Stage*.

Again, confider it in another View: How is it poffible
that any one fhould delight in the *Stage*, but thro' a Defect
in Piety? For is not the Stage guilty of Impurity, Prophanenefs, Blafphemy, and Immorality? Now tho' People may
differ about the Degree in which they will make this Charge,
yet all muft own it in fome degree. Now if the Charge be
but true in *any degree*, muft there not be a Want of Piety
in thofe that can partake of an Entertainment chargeable with
Impurity, *Prophanenefs*, and *Immorality*? If People were fo
pious that they could not bear fuch an Entertainment as this;
it nothing could perfuade them to be prefent at it, this would
be no Proof that they were Saints; for to abhor an Entertainment loaded with fo much Guilt, is but a fmall Inftance
of an advanc'd Piety. But furely, if they can not only bear
it, but be pleas'd with it, it is Proof enough that their Hearts
want feveral Degrees of Piety, which become Chriftians.
Befides, can pious Perfons, who ufe the *Stage*, tell you of
any *one Play* for this forty or fifty Years, that has been free
from *wild* Rant, *immodeft* Paffions, and *prophane* Language?
Muft they not therefore be defective in Piety, who partake
of a Diverfion that is at *no time* free from this Guilt in fome
degree or other? But fuppofing there were fuch a thing as an
innocent Play once or twice in an Age, (which is like fuppofing *innocent* Luft, *fober* Rant, or harmlefs Prophanenefs)
could this make it at all allowable for pious Perfons to ufe the
Stage? Could this be any Proof that Perfons of real Piety
might take pleafure in it? For could it be confiftent with an
enliven'd Piety to ufe a Diverfion, which in its *common ordinary* State is full of monftrous Impiety and Prophanenefs,
becaufe it fometimes happen'd in a Number of Years, that
it might be innocent for a *Day* or *two*? But even this does
not happen. The Stage never has *one* innocent Play; not
one

one can be produced that ever you faw acted in *either Houfe*,
but what abounds with *Thoughts*, *Paffions* and *Language* contrary to Religion. Is there therefore any Rafhnefs or Severity in faying, That Perfons who ufe a Diverfion, which in
its *ordinary* State is full of monftrous Wickednefs and Impiety, and in its *beft* State never free from Variety of Sin, to
fay that fuch Perfons muft be defective in Piety? How can
we know any thing with Clearnefs and Evidence, if we don't
know this to be clear and evident? For furely it is a neceffary Part of Piety to abhor Lewdnefs, Immorality, or Prophanenefs, where-ever they are; but they who are fo pious as
not to be able to be pleas'd where any of thofe are, have a
Piety that will not permit them ever to fee a Play.

There is no Doctrine of our Bleffed Saviour, that more
concerns all Chriftians, or is more effential to their Salvation
than this: *Bleffed are the pure in heart, for they fhall fee God.*
Now take the *Stage* in its beft State, when fome admir'd
Tragedy is upon it, are the *extravagant Paffions* of diftracted
Lovers, the *impure Ravings* of inflam'd Heroes, the *Joys* and
Torments of Love, and *grofs Defcriptions* of Luft; are the *indecent* Actions, the *amorous* Tranfports, the *wanton Addrefs*
of the Actors, which make fo great a Part of the *moft fober*
and *modeft* Tragedies; are thefe things confiftent with this
Chriftian Doctrine of *Purity of Heart?* You may as well
imagine, that *Murder* and *Rapine* are confiftent with *Charity*
and *Meeknefs*.

It is therefore as neceffary, as reafonable, and as confiftent
with Chriftian Charity, to tell *Levis*, that his Ufe and Delight in the *Stage* is a certain Proof of his want of Piety, as
to tell the fame thing to a malicious, intemperate, or revenge-
ful Perfon. Some People who are guilty of perfonal Vices
may have fome Violence of Temptation, fome natural Diforder to plead in their Excufe; they perhaps may be fo tender as to defire to conceal them, and be afraid to encourage
others in the like Practices; but the Ufe and Encouragement
of the *Stage* has no Excufes of this kind; it has no *Infirmity*,
Surprize, or *Violence* of Temptation to appeal to; it fhews no
Tendernefs of Mind, or *Concern* for others, but is a deliberate,
continued, open and publick Declaration in favour of *Lewdnefs*, *Immorality* and *Prophanenefs*. Let any one but collect,
not all the Wickednefs that has appear'd on the Stage fince
he firft ufed it, but only fo much as paffes there in *any one*
Seafon, and then he will fee what a dreadful Load of Guilt
he has brought upon himfelf. For furely no one can be fo
weak

weak as to imagine, that he can use and encourage a wicked
Entertainment, without making himself a *full Sharer* of all its
Wickedness.

Archbishop *Tillotson* treats the Stage in this manner. ‘ I
‘ shall now speak a few Words concerning *Plays*, which as
‘ they are now order'd amongst us, are a *mighty Reproach* to
‘ the Age and Nation. ——As now the Stage is, they are
‘ *intolerable*, and not fit to be permitted in a *civiliz'd*, much
‘ less a *Christian* Nation. They do most *notoriously* minister
‘ to Infidelity and Vice. ——And therefore I do not see how
‘ any Person *pretending* to Sobriety and Virtue, and especially
‘ to the *pure* and *holy* Religion of our Blessed Saviour, can
‘ without *great Guilt*, and open *Contradiction* to his holy Pro-
‘ fession, be present at such lewd and immodest Plays, as too
‘ many do ; who yet would take it very ill to be shut out of
‘ the Community of Christians, as they would most cer-
‘ tainly have been in the first and purest Ages of Christia-
‘ nity *.

Here let it be observ'd, that this Archbishop, who has generally been reckon'd eminent for his *Moderation* and *gentle*
manner of treating every thing, says of Plays, that they are a
mighty Reproach to the Nation; that they are *intolerable*, and
not fit to be permitted in a *Civiliz'd*, much less a *Christian
Nation*; that they *notoriously* minister to *Infidelity* and *Vice*.

Now this, I suppose, is as high a Charge, as he would have
brought against the worst Articles of *Popery*. If I have said,
that People cannot use the *Stage* without being defective in
Piety ; I have not said it in a declaiming way, but have af-
serted it from Variety of plain Arguments : But this great Man,
so much admired for his *tender* Remarks upon *Persons* and
Things, goes much farther. He does not say, that People of
real and advanc'd Piety cannot use the *Stage* ; but he makes
it inconsistent with so much as *pretending to Sobriety and Vir-*
tue, much less the *Purity* and *holy Religion* of our blessed Saviour. He does not say, that such People cannot be Excellent and Exemplary Christians, or that they must be defective
in Piety ; but he charges them with *great Guilt*, and *open Con-*
tradiction to their Holy Religion ; and assures them, that if
they had liv'd in the *first* and *purest* Ages of Christianity, they
would have been excommunicated.

***

* *Serm. upon corrupt Communication.*

I have appeal'd to this *great Name,* for no other End, but to prevent the Charge of Uncharitablenefs. For furely, if fuch an eminent Inftance of a *charitable* and *gentle* Spirit can roundly affirm, that the Ufe of fuch a *Stage* as ours is an *open Contradiction* to Chriftianity, and fuch a fcandalous Offence, as would certainly have been punifh'd in the firft and pureft Ages of the Church, by the dreadful Punifhment of Excommunication; furely it can be no Proof of an *uncharitable Spirit* in me, that I fhew by Variety of Arguments, that the Ufe of fuch a *Stage* cannot confift with the true Spirit of Chriftianity; but that there muft be *fome Defect* in their Piety, who are able to ufe it.

Jucunda refolves in great Chearfulnefs to hear no Arguments againft the *Stage :* She fays it can be but a *fmall Sin;* and, confidering the Wickednefs of the Age, that Perfon is in a very good State, that is only guilty of going to Plays. Defire her ever fo often only to confider the plaineft Argument in the World; fhe puts all off with only this Reply, *God fend I may have no greater Sin to anfwer for, than feeing a Play!*

Jucunda thinks a Clergyman would do better, to infift only upon the Material Parts of Religion; and not put fo much Strefs upon Things that are only *Diverfions;* left by making Religion to contradict People in every thing, Religion it felf fhould be brought into diflike. *Jucunda* defires, that fhe may be inftructed in fome greater Things, than the Sinfulnefs of going to a *Play;* for fhe is refolved to hear no more of that.

But pray, *Jucunda,* confider all that you have here faid. You fay, it can be but a *fmall Sin.* How is it that you know it is but a *fmall Sin?* What care have you taken to underftand its true Magnitude? You fhut your Eyes, and ftop your Ears, and refolve againft all Information about it; and then call it a *fmall Sin.* But fuppofe it were but a *fmall Sin;* is that a Reafon why you fhould be guilty of it? Does the Smalnefs of Sins recommend them to your Choice? Our bleffed Saviour faith, * *If thy foot offend thee, cut it off; it is better for thee to enter halt into life, than having two feet, to be caft into hell. And if thine eye offend thee, pluck it out;*

---

* Mark ix. 47.

F   *it*

*it is better for thee to enter into the kingdom of God with one
eye, than having two eyes, to be cast into hell-fire.* Now this
paffage, I fuppofe, does not mean, If thou art guilty of fome
great Sin, either of *Murder, Perjury,* or the like, thou muft
cut them off. For, the Comparifon of a *Foot* and an *Eye,*
muft fignify fomething that is not directly finful in it felf, but
only dangerous in its Ufe; as it fets us too near to fome Sins,
or is become too full of Temptation. Yet fuch ways of Life
as thefe, which are only dangerous, and expofe our Virtue to
too great a Hazard, however pleafant and ufeful, (tho' like
an Eye, or Foot) are yet to be entirely cut off, that we may
not fall into Hell-fire. Can it be fuppos'd that *Jucunda* is of
this Religion, who pleafes her felf with a Diverfion, becaufe
it is but a *fmall Sin?* Will fhe ever think of faving her felf,
by cutting off a *Foot,* or plucking out an *Eye?*

Indeed, to talk of a *fmall Sin,* is like talking of a *fmall
Law* of God : For, as there is no Law of God, but is a
great one, becaufe it comes from God ; fo every Sin, as it
is a Tranfgreffion of fome Law of God, muft needs be a
great one. There may be Sins that have a fmaller degree of
Guilt; becaufe they may be committed thro' *Infirmity, Ignorance,* or *Surprize*; but no Sin is fmall, that is either carelefly
or wilfully continued in. If it be a Sin therefore to ufe the
Stage, it cannot be a *fmall one* ; becaufe it has none of thofe
Circumftances which render a Sin a fmall one. It becomes
a very great one to *Jucunda* ; becaufe fhe carelefly and wilfully refolves to continue in it, merely for the fake of a little
Diverfion.

Let *Jucunda* confider again, what fhe means by wifhing
that fhe may have no greater Sin to anfwer for than going
to a Play. It is a Wifh that is filly in itfelf, becaufe fhe is
not to wifh to dye in fmall Sins, but in a perfect Repentance
and Abhorrence of all kind of Sin; but it is much fillier ftill,
when it is given as a Reafon for going to a *Play.* For it is
faying, *I expect to dye guilty of greater Sins than of going to
a Play, and therefore there is no Occafion to forbear from that.*
Now if fhe underftands herfelf fhe muft know, that this is the
plain Meaning of her Words. Yet who that underftands any
thing of Religion, or that has any Defire of Holinefs, can
talk at this rate? It is a Language that is fitter for an *Atheift,*
than for a Perfon that is but *half* a Chriftian. If a Tradef-
man that allows himfelf only to lye in the Prices of his
Goods, fhould content himfelf with faying, *God fend I may
have*

4

have no greater Sins to answer for, no one would suppose him to be much concern'd about Religion. Yet as many Chriftian Reafons might be produced to fhew thefe Lies to be but fmall Sins, as to fhew that the Ufe of the Stage is but a *fmall Sin.*

Jucunda would have a *Clergyman* infift upon the moft material Parts of Religion, and not lay fo much ftrefs upon things that are only Diverfions. I am of your mind, *Jucunda,* that a Clergyman ought to infift upon the moft material Parts of Religion; but then it does not follow, that he muft not lay much ftrefs upon things that are *Diverfions.* For as fomething that is called a Diverfion may be entirely finful, fo if this fhould happen, it is as neceffary for a Clergyman to call all Chriftians from it, as it is neceffary to exhort them to keep the Commandments. Religion feems to have as little to do with *Trades,* as with *Diverfions*; yet if a Trade be fet up, that is in its own Nature wicked, there is nothing more material in Religion, than to declare the Neceffity of forfaking fuch an Employment. But after all, *Jucunda,* the moft effential, and moft *material* Parts of Religion are fuch as relate to *common Life,* fuch as alter our Ways of living, fuch as give Rules to all our Actions, and are the Meafure of all our Conduct, whether in Bufinefs or Diverfion. Nothing is fo important in Religion to you, as that which makes you fober and wife, holy and heavenly-minded in the whole Courfe of your Life. But you are for fuch *material Parts* of Religion, as fhould only diftinguifh you from a *Jew* or an *Infidel,* but make no Difference in common Life betwixt you and *Fops* and *Coquets.* You are for a Religion that confifts in Modes and Forms of Worfhip, that is ty'd to *Times* and *Places,* that only takes up a little of your time on *Sunday,* and leaves you all the Week to do as you pleafe. But all this, *Jucunda,* is nothing. The Scripture hath not faid in vain, *He that is in Chrift is a new Creature.* All the Law and the Gofpel are in vain to you; all Sacraments, Devotions, Doctrines and Ordinances are to no purpofe, unlefs they make you this *new Creature* in all the Actions of your Life. He teaches you the moft material Parts of Religion, who teaches you to be of a *religious Spirit* in every thing that you do, who teaches you to eat and drink, to labour and reft, to converfe and divert yourfelf in fuch degrees, and to fuch Ends, as beft promote a pious Life.

If *Sots* and *Gluttons* fhould defire a *Clergyman* to infift upon the moft material Parts of Religion, and not lay fo great

a ftrefs

a ſtreſs upon *Gluttony* and *Intemperance*, which are things that only relate to *eating* and *drinking*; they would ſhew that they underſtood Religion as well as *Jucunda*. For every one muſt ſee, that *ſome Diverſions* may as much diſorder the Heart, and be as contrary to Religion, as *Gluttony* and *Intemperance*. And perhaps as many People have liv'd and dy'd unaffected with Religion, thro' a Courſe of *Diverſions* and *Pleaſures*, as thro' Gluttony and Intemperance.

If it diſpleaſes People to be told, that Religion is to pre-ſcribe Rules to their Diverſions, they are as unreaſonable as thoſe are, who are diſpleas'd that Religion ſhould preſcribe Rules to their Tempers, and Paſſions, and Inclinations. For as Diverſions are only the Gratifications of our Tempers, ſo if Religion is to forbear us in our Diverſions, it is to forbear our Tempers, Paſſions and Inclinations. But the Truth is, we ought to be more religiouſly cautious and watchful about our Diverſions, than any other Part of common Life; not only becauſe they take ſuch deep hold of us, but becauſe they have no neceſſary Foundation in Nature, but are our own Inventions. *Trade* and Buſineſs, tho' they are neceſſary for great Ends of Life, are yet to be ſubject to the ſtricteſt Rules of Religion; ſurely therefore *Diverſions*, which are but like ſo many *Blanks* in Life, that are only invented to get rid of Time, ſurely ſuch things ought of all others to have no *mixture* of any thing that is ſinful in them. For if the thing it ſelf be hardly pardonable, ſurely it muſt be a high Crime to add to it the Sin of doing it in a ſinful manner. For as Diverſions are at beſt only Methods of loſing Time, the moſt innocent have ſomething in them that ſeems to want a Pardon; but if we cannot be content with ſuch as only paſs away our Hours, unleſs they gratify our diſorder'd Paſſions, we are like thoſe who are not content to ſleep away their time, unleſs they can add the Pleaſure of ſinful Dreams.

Jucunda therefore is much miſtaken, if ſhe thinks that Religion has nothing to do with her Diverſions, for there is nothing that requires a more religious Exactneſs than they do. If we are wrong in them, it is the ſame thing as if we are wrong in our Religion, or ſinful in our Buſineſs. Nay, Sin in our Diverſions is leſs excuſable, and perhaps does us more harm than in any thing elſe. For ſuch as our Diverſions are, ſuch are we our ſelves. If Religion therefore is to have any Power over us; if it is to enter into our Hearts, and alter and reform the State of our Souls, the greateſt Work that it has to

to do, is to remove us from such Pleasures and Ways of
Life, as nourish and support a wrong State of our Souls.

If dying Sinners that go out of the World under a Load
of Guilt could see what brought them into that State, it
would often be found, that all their Sins, and Impieties, and
Neglects of Duty, were solely owing to their Diversions;
and perhaps were they to live their Lives over again, there
would be no other possible way of living better than they
had done, but by renouncing such ways of Life, as were
only look'd upon as Diversions and Amusements.

People of Fashion and Quality have great Advantage above
the Vulgar; their Condition and Education gives them a
Liveliness and Brightness of Parts, from whence one might
justly expect a more exalted Virtue. How comes it then,
that we see as ill *Morals*, as open *Impiety*, as little *religious
Wisdom*, and as great *Disorders* among them, as among the
most rude, uneducated Part of the World? It is because the
Politeness of their Lives, their Course of Diversions and A-
musements, and their Ways of spending their time, as much
extinguishes the *Wisdom* and *Light* of Religion, as the Gross-
ness and Ignorance of the dullest Part of the World. A
poor Creature that is doom'd to a stupid Conversation, that
sees nothing but *Drudgery*, and *Eating, Drinking* and *Sleeping*,
is as likely to have his Soul aspire to God, and aim at an
exalted Virtue, as another that is always in the Brightness and
Gayety of polite Pleasures. It is the same thing whether the
good Seed be burnt up with the Heat and Brightness of the
Sun, or be lost in *Mud*. Many Persons that live and dye in
a *Mine*, that are confin'd to Drudgery and Darkness, are just
so fatally destroy'd by their way of Life, as others that live
in a Circle of Pleasures and polite Engagements are destroy'd
by their way of Life. Every one sees and owns the Effects
of such a gross way of Life; it is not usual to expect any
thing wise, or holy, or truly great, from Persons that live
and dye digging *Coals*. But then it is not enough consider'd,
that there are other Ways of Life of a contrary Appearance,
that as certainly and unavoidably produce the same Effects.
For a Heart that is devoted to *polite* Pleasures, that is
taken up with a Succession of vain and corrupt *Diversions*,
that is employ'd in *Assemblies, Gaming, Plays, Balls*, and such
like Business of a *genteel* Life, is as much dispos'd of, and taken as far out of the way of true Religion, and a divine and
holy Life, as if it had been shut up in a *Mine*. These are
plain and certain Truths, if there is any thing plain and cer-

tain,

tain, either in the Nature of Religion, or the Nature of Man. Who expects Piety from a *Tapster*, that lives amongst the Rudeness, Noise and Intemperance of an *Alehouse*? Who expects Christian Holiness from a *Juggler*, that goes about with his *Cups* and *Balls*? Yet why is not this as reasonable, as to expect Piety and Christian Holiness from a *fine Gentleman* that lives at a *Gaming-Table*? Is there any more reason to look for Christian Fortitude, divine Tempers, or religious Greatness of Mind in this State of Life? Had such a one been born in low Life with the same turn of Mind, it had in all probability fix'd him in an *Ale-house*, or furnish'd him with *Cups* and *Balls*.

The sober, honest Employments of Life, and the reasonable Cares of every Condition in the World, makes it sufficiently difficult for People to live enough to God, and to act with such holy and wise Tempers as Religion requireth. But, if we make our Wealth and Fortunes the Gratifications of idle and disorder'd Passions, we may make it as difficult to be saved in a State of *Politeness* and *Genteelity*, as in the *basest* Occupations of Life.

Religion requires a steady, resolute Use of our best Reason, and an earnest Application to God for the Light and Assistance of his Holy Spirit.

It is only this watchful Temper, that is full of Attention to every thing that is right and good, that watches over our Minds, and guards our Hearts, that loves Reason, that desires Wisdom, and constantly calls upon God for the Light and Joy of his holy Spirit; it is this Temper alone that can preserve us in any true State of Christian Holiness. There is no Possibility of having our Minds strengthen'd and fix'd in wise and reasonable Judgments, or our Hearts full of good and regular Motions; but by living in such a *way of Life*, as assists and improves our Reason, and prepares and disposes us to receive the Spirit of God. This is as certainly the *one only* way to Holiness, as there is but one God that is Holy. Religion can no more subsist in a trifling, vain Spirit, that lives by Humour and Fancy, that is full of Levity and Impertinence, wandring from Passion to Passion, giddy with silly Joys, and burden'd with impertinent Cares, it can no more subsist with this State of the Soul, than it can dwell in a Heart *devoted* to Sin.

Any way of Life therefore that darkens our Minds, that misemploys our Reason, that fills us with a trifling Spirit, that disorders our Passions, that separates us from the Spirit of God,

God, is the same certain Road to Destruction; whether it arise from stupid *Sensuality*, rude *Ignorance*, or polite *Pleasures*. Had any one therefore the Power of an *Apostle*, or the Tongue of an *Angel*, he could not employ it better, than in censuring and condemning those ways of Life, which *Wealth, Corruption*, and *Politeness* have brought amongst us. We, indeed, only call them Diversions; but they do the whole Work of *Idolatry* and *Infidelity*, and fill People with so much Blindness and Hardness of Heart, that they neither live by Reason, nor feel the want of it; but are content to play away their Lives, as regardless of every Thing that is wise, and holy, and divine, as if they were mere *Birds*, or *Animals*; and as thoughtless of Death, and Judgment, and Eternity, as if these were Things that had no Relation to human Life.

Now, all this Blindness and Hardness of Heart is owing to that way of Life, which People of Fortune generally fall into. It is not gross Sins, it is not *Murder*, or *Adultery*; but it is their *Genteelity* and *Politeness*, that destroys them : It fills them with such Passions and Pleasures, as quite extinguish the gentle Light of Reason and Religion. For, if Religion requireth a sober Turn of Mind; if we cannot be reasonable, but by subduing and governing our blind Tempers and Passions; if the most necessary Enjoyments of Life require great Caution and Sobriety, that our Souls be not made earthly and sensual by them; what way of Life can so waste and destroy our Souls, what can so strengthen our Passions, and disorder our Hearts, as a Life of such Diversions, Entertainments and Pleasures, as are the *Business* of great Part of the World ?

If Religion is to reform our Souls, to deliver us from the Corruption of our Nature, to restore the divine Image, and fill us with such Tempers of Purity and Perfection, as may fit us for the Eternal Enjoyment of God; what is the polite Part of the World a doing? For how can any one more renounce such a Religion as this; how can he more resist the Grace of God, and hinder the Recovery of the Divine Image, than by living in a Succession of such Enjoyments, as the Generality of People of Fashion are devoted to ? For no one, who uses the *Stage*, has any more Reason to expect to grow in the Grace of God, or to be enlighten'd and purify'd by his Holy Spirit, than he that never uses any Devotion. So that it is not to be wonder'd at, if the Spirit and Power of Religion is wanted, where People so live, as neither to be fit to

receive,

receive, nor able to co-operate with the Affiftance and Light of God's Holy Spirit.

We are taught, that *Charity covereth the multitude of fins*; and, that *alms fhall purge away fins*. Now, let this teach fome People how to judge of the Guilt of thofe Gifts and Contributions, which are given contrary to Charity. I don't mean fuch Money, as is idly and impertinently fquander'd away; but fuch *Gifts* and *Contributions*, as are to fupport People in a wicked Life. For, this is fo great a Contradiction to Charity, that it muft certainly have Effects contrary to it : It muft as much cover our *Virtues*, as Charity covereth our *Sins*.

It is no ftrange Thing, to hear of *Ladies* taking care of a *Benefit-Night* in the Play-Houfe. But furely, they never reflect upon what they are doing. For if there is any Bleffing that attends Charity, there muft as great a Curfe attend. fuch Liberalities, as are to reward People for their Wickednefs, and make them happy and profperous in an unchriftian Profeffion. How can they expect the Bleffings of God, or to have their Virtues and Charities placed to their Account; when they have blotted them out, by their Contributions and Generofities to the moft open Enemies of the Purity and Holinefs of Chrift's Religion? He that is thus with the Play-Houfe, is moft openly againft God; and is as certainly oppofing Religion, as he that rewards thofe that labour in the Caufe of Infidelity.

It is no uncharitable Affertion, to affirm, that a Player cannot be a living Member of Chrift, or in a true State of Grace, till he renounces his Profeffion, with a fincere and deep Repentance. Chriftianity no more allows fuch Plays and Players as ours are, than it allows the groffeft Vices. They are Objects of no other Charity, or Kindnefs, than fuch as may reduce them to a fincere Repentance. What a Guilt therefore do they bring upon themfelves, who make Players their Favourites, and publick Objects of their Care and Generofity; who cannot be in the Favour of God, till they ceafe to be fuch as they encourage them to be; till they renounce that Life, for which they efteem and reward them?

When an Object of *Diftrefs* is offer'd to People, it is common to fee them very fcrupulous in their Charity; they feem to think there may be fuch a thing as a blameable Charity; they defire to know whether the Perfon be worthy, whether his Diftrefs is not owing to his Follies and Extravagancies; that they may not relieve fuch a one, as ought to feel the

Punifh-

Punishment of his Follies. But what muft we fay to thefe things, if thofe who are thus nice in their *Alms*, are yet un-reafonable in their *Generofities*; who are afraid of affifting a poor Man, till every thing can be faid in his Favour; and yet eager to make another rich, who is only recommended by his Follies? What fhall we fay to thefe things, if Perfons who have fo many Rules to govern and reftrain their Pity to poor Men, have yet no Rules to govern their Liberalities and Kindnefs to Libertines? If they fhall have a *Benefit-Night* upon their hands, not to relieve the Poverty, but to reward the *Merit* of a Player, that he may have the Subfiftence of a *Gentleman* from Chriftians, for a way of Life that would be a Reproach to a fober Heathen? Shall we reckon this amongft our fmall Offences? Is this a pardonable Inftance of the Weaknefs of human Nature? Is it not rather an undeniable Proof, that Chriftianity has no hold of our Reafon and Judgment? And that we muft be born again from fuch a State of Heart as this, before we can enter into the Spirit of Chriftianity?

I have now only one thing to defire of the Reader, Not that he would like and approve of thefe Reflexions, but that he will not fuffer himfelf to diflike or condemn them, till he has put his Arguments into Form, and knows how many Doctrines of Scripture he can bring againft thofe things that I have afferted. So far as he can fhew that I have reafoned wrong, or miftook the Doctrine of Scripture, fo far he has a Right to cenfure. But *general Diflikes* are mere *Tempers*, as blind as *Paffions*, and are always the ftrongeft where Reafons are moft wanted. If People will diflike, becaufe they will, and condemn Doctrines, only becaufe it fuits better with their *Tempers* and *Practices*, than to confider and underftand them to be true; they act by the fame Spirit of *Popery*, as is moft remarkable in the *loweft Bigots*, who are refolute in a *general Diflike* of all *Proteftant* Doctrines, without fuffering themfelves to confider and underftand upon what Truth they are founded.

I can eafily imagine, that fome People will cenfure thefe Doctrines, as proceeding from a *rigid*, *uncharitable* Temper, becaufe they feem to condemn fo great a Part of the World. Had I wrote a Treatife againft *Covetoufnefs* or *Intemperance*, it had certainly condemned great Part of the World; but furely he muft have ftrangely forgot himfelf, that fhould make that a Reafon of accufing me of an uncharitable Temper.

G   Such

Such People fhould confider alfo, that a Man cannot affert the Doctrines of Chriftian *Charity* and *Meeknefs* themfelves, without condemning a very great Part of the World. But would it be an Inftance of an uncharitable Spirit, to preach up the Neceffity of an univerfal Charity, becaufe it might condemn a very great Part of the World? And if the *Holinefs* of Chriftianity cannot be afferted, without condemning the Pleafures and Entertainments of the fafhionable Part of the World, is there any more Uncharitablenefs in this, than in afferting the Doctrine of univerfal Love? Does this any more fhew an *unchriftian*, *rigid* Spirit, than when the beloved Apoftle faid, *All that is in the World, the Luft of the Flefh, the Luft of the Eyes, and the Pride of Life, is not of the Father, but is of the World?*

But I fhall not now confider any more Objections, but leave all that I have faid to the Confcience and Reafon of every Perfon. Let him but make Reafon and Religion the Meafure of his Judgment, and then he is as favourable to me as I defire him to be.

It is very common and natural for People to ftruggle hard, and be loth to own any thing to be wrong that they have long practis'd. Many People will fee fo much Truth in thefe Arguments againft the *Stage*, that they will wifh in their own Minds that they had always forbore it. But then finding that they cannot affent to thefe Arguments without taking a great deal of blame to themfelves, they will find ftrong Inclinations to condemn the plaineft Reafonings, rather than condemn themfelves. Let but a Perfon forget that he has any Guilt in relation to the *Stage*, let him but fuppofe that he has never been there, and that he will go or ftay away, juft as he finds Reafon, when he has examin'd all that can be faid againft it; let a Man but put himfelf in this State of Mind, and then he will fee all the Arguments againft the Stage, as plain and convincing, as any that can be brought againft the groffeft Vices.

If we could look into the Minds of the feveral Sorts of Readers, we fhould fee how differently People are affected with Arguments, according to the State that they are in. We fhould fee how thofe, who have never ufed the *Stage*, confent with the whole Force of their Minds, and fee the Certainty and Plainnefs of every Argument againft it. We fhould fee others ftruggling and contending againft all Conviction, in proportion to the Ufe that they have made of the *Stage*. Thofe that have been its Friends and Advocates, and conftant Admirers, will

will hate the very Name of a Book that is wrote against it, and will condemn every Argument, without knowing what it is. Those who have used the *Stage* much, tho' in a less degree than this, will perhaps vouchsafe to read a Book against it; but they will read with Fear ; they will strive not to be convinced, and be angry at every Argument, for proving so much as it does. Others, that have used the *Stage* in the most moderate degree, have yet great Prejudices : They perhaps will own, that the *Stage* is blameable ; and that it is very well to perswade People from it : But then, these People will not assent to the whole Truth. They will not condemn the Stage, as they ought ; because having been there sometimes themselves, it suits better with their own Practice only to condemn it in the general, than to declare it to be sinful in such a degree, as should condemn those who ever use it.

These are the several Difficulties, which this Treatise has to contend with : It is to oppose an Evil Practice, and charge it with *such a Degree* of Guilt, as few can consent to, without taking some Part of that Guilt to themselves.

I have mention'd these several Degrees of Prejudice, to put People upon suspecting themselves, and trying the State of their Hearts. For, the only way to be wise and reasonable, is to suspect our selves, and put Questions to our selves in private, which only our own Hearts can answer. Let any one who reads this Treatise, ask himself, whether he reads it, as he reads those Things which have no Relation to himself ? When he reads a Treatise against *Image-Worship*, or Prayers to *Saints*, he knows that he attends to the whole Force of the Arguments ; that he desires to see them in their full Strength, and to comprehend every Evil that they charge upon it. Now every one can tell, whether he reads this Treatise with this Temper ; or whether he comes heavily to it, and unwilling to be convinced by it. If this is his State, he ought to charge himself with all that, which he charges upon the most absurd and perverse People in Life. For it is only this Temper, an *Inclination* not to be convinc'd, that makes People so *positive* and *obstinate* in Ways and Opinions, that appear so shocking to all reasonable Men. It is this Temper, that makes the *Jew*, the *Infidel*, the *Papist* and the *Fanatick*, of every kind. And he that is not reasonable enough to read impartially a Treatise against the *Stage*, has no Reason to think, that his Mind is in better Order than theirs is, who cannot freely consider a Book that is wrote against the *Worship of Images*, and Prayers to *Saints*.

There

There is but one Thing for reasonable People to do in this Case; Either to answer all the Arguments here produced against the *Stage*; or to yield to the Truth of them, and regulate their Lives according to them. Our Conduct in this Affair is far from being a small Matter. I have produced no Arguments, but such as are taken from the most Essential Parts of Religion: If therefore there is any Truth in them, the Use of the *Stage* is certainly to be reckon'd amongst *great* and *flagrant* Sins.

I have now only to advise those, who are hereby made sensible of the Necessity of renouncing the *Stage*, that they will act in this Case, as they expect that others should act in Cases of the like nature. That they will not think it sufficient to forbear the Stage themselves, but be instrumental as far as they can in keeping others from it; and that they will think it as necessary to make this amends for their former Compliance and ill Example, as it is necessary to make *Restitution* in cases of Injury. The Cause of Religion, the Honour of God, the Good of their Neighbour, and the Peace and Satisfaction of their own Minds, necessarily requires this at their Hands. For as no one can tell how far his Example may have influenc'd others, and how many People may have been injur'd by his means; so it is absolutely necessary, that he do as much good as he can, by a better Example, and make his own Change of Life a Means of reducing others to the same State of Amendment.

F I N I S.

THE
STAGE
DEFENDED,

FROM

SCRIPTURE, REASON, EXPERIENCE, and the Common Sense of MANKIND, for Two Thousand Years.

Occasion'd by Mr. *Law*'s late Pamphlet against STAGE-ENTERTAINMENTS.

In a LETTER to ******

By Mr. *DENNIS*.

LONDON:

Printed for N. BLANDFORD, at the *London-Gazette*, *Charing Cross*; and sold by J. PEELE, at *Locke's-Head* in *Pater-noster-Row*. MDCCXXVI.

(Price One Shilling.)

The STAGE defended, *&c.*

To —— *Efq*;

S I R,

HEN you defire to know my Sentiments concerning Mr. *Law*'s late Pamphlet againſt the Stage, you make a Requeſt, which 'tis not ſo eaſy for me to
ſatisfy as you may perhaps imagine :
For I really never was ſo much at a
Loſs to know what an Author meant.
Sometimes I am inclined to think him in good earneſt ;
and ſometimes I believe, that there are Grounds to ſuſpect, that he deſign'd this whole Pamphlet for nothing
but a ſpiritual Banter ; for there ſeems to me to be a Neceſſity of believing, either that a Clergyman, as Mr. *Law*
is, ſhould be profoundly ignorant of the ſacred Writings,
a Man of Letters of the Nature of Dramatick Poems,
and one who had liv'd long enough in the World to have
ſome Experience of the preſent State of Religion, and
Virtue, and Vice, among us ; or a Neceſſity of conclud-

B   ing,

ing, that while Mr. *Law* is declaiming with fo much furious Zeal againft the Stage and Players, he is all that while acting a Part, and fhewing himfelf a great Comedian.

When Mr. *Law* is putting Idolatry and frequenting the Playhoufe upon an equal Foot, he feems to be playing a Part; for he cannot but know, that St. *Paul* was of another Mind, who when he was at *Athens*, the very Source of Dramatick Poetry, faid a great deal publickly againft their Idolatry, but not one Word againft their Stage. When he was afterwards at *Corinth*, as little did he fay againft theirs : For St. *Paul*, who was educated in all the Learning of the *Grecians*, who had read all their Poets, who in the vjth Chapter of the *Acts*, Ver. 28, quotes *Aratus*, and *Epimenides*, in the firft Chapter of his Epiftle to *Titus*, Ver. 10, could not but have read all their noble Dramatick Poems; and yet has been fo far from fpeaking one Word againft them, that he has made ufe of them for the Inftruction and Converfion of Mankind. And when afterwards he wrote his Firft Epiftle to the *Corinthians*, he did not fcruple, for their Inftruction, to make ufe of an *Athenian* Play; for all the World knows, that *Evil Communications corrupt Good Manners*, 1 *Cor.* xv. 33. is taken from an *Athenian* Dramatick Poet. Does Mr. *Law* believe that that Epiftle, and confequently that Verfe, was dictated by the Holy Ghoft or not ? Can Mr. *Law* believe, that St. *Paul* was guided by the Spirit of God to make Choice of that Verfe for the Inftruction, and Converfion of the *Corinthians* ? And can he believe at the fame Time, that the Theatre, as he more than once declares

clares it, is the Temple of the Devil ? If any one should affirm, That St. *Paul* was guided by the Spirit of God, to take a Verse from the Temple of the Devil, would it not be such horrid Blasphemy as would make even the Blood of the most profligate of all Players to curdle within the Miscreant's Veins. But if St. *Paul* had in the least believed, that the *Athenian* Stage was the Sink of Sin and Corruption, as Mr. *Law* says every Stage is, he would not have fail'd to reproach them with it, in order to check the spreading Evil. He who dares talk openly and boldly against the National Religion of a People, may very well venture to condemn their Vices and evil Customs. But St. *Paul* not only says nothing at all against Dramatick Poetry, but makes use of it for the Conversion and Reformation of Mankind. Now I would fain know, if quoting a Dramatick Poet, without giving the least Caution against the Stage, be not a downright Approbation of Dramatick Poetry, and establishing the Stage by no lesser an Authority than that of the Spirit of God himself.

If we look into the Old Testament, we shall find, that the Kings of *Israel* and *Judah*, they and their Reigns, were declared righteous or wicked, according as those Kings were Idolaters or not Idolaters ; and that no Sin whatever was reckon'd so abominable as Idolatry. *Solomon*, who had seven hundred Wives, had no less than three hundred Concubines ; and yet when God threatened to rend Ten Tribes of his Subjects from him, it was only for his Idolatry, *because he had forsaken God, and had worshipped Ashtoreth the Goddess of the Sidonians, Chemosh*

the

the God *of the* Moabites, *and* Milcom *the* God *of the* Chil- *dren of* Ammon, 1 Kings xj. *For it came to pafs, that when* Solomon *was old, his* Wives *turned away his Heart after other Gods, and his Heart was not perfect with the* Lord *his* God, *as was the Heart of* David *his Father,* ibid. Ver. 4. Now *David* committed Adultery with *Bath- fheba,* and murdered her Husband *Uriah ;* yet thefe Sins that were of fo flagrant a Nature that they brought a Plague upon *Ifrael,* were venial, compared to Idolatry. They brought, indeed, a Plague upon the People, but they depofed the King from no Part of his Subjects, as the Idolatry of *Solomon* did his Son *Rehoboam.* In fhort, Idolatry is by fo much more criminal than the Tranfgref- fion of any other divine Commandment, as the Attempt to depofe a King and to fet up a Pretender, is a Crime of a higher Nature than the Breach of any other human Law.

As it is hard to imagine, that Mr. *Law* fhould be ig- norant of what has been faid above, it gave me juft Caufe to fufpect his Sincerity : But when I came to the Paffage which he quotes from Archbifhop *Tillotfon,* in the 38th Page of his Pamplet, I found that he prevaricated fo vilely in it, that the Hypocrify became immediately ma- nifeft : For he has omitted the former Part of the Paffage, becaufe it makes directly againft him. It is as follows :

To fpeak againft them (viz. Plays) *in general, may be thought too fevere, and that which the prefent Age cannot fo well brook, and would not perhaps be fo juft and reafon- able, becaufe it is very poffible they might be fo framed, and*
governed

governed by such Rules, as not only to be innocent and di-
verting, but instructive and useful, to put some Vices and
Follies out of Countenance, which cannot perhaps be so de-
cently reproved, nor so effectually exposed and corrected any
other Way. All this, as I have said above, he has pur-
posely omitted, because it makes point blank against him.

For after he has told us, in this blessed Pamphlet, *That*
the Playhouse is the Temple of the Devil, a more delightful
Habitation for him than ever any Temple that he had in the
Heathen World, where Impurity and Filthiness, immodest
Songs, prophane Rants, Lust, and Passions, entertain the
Audience, a Place, the peculiar Pleasure of the Devil, where
all they who go, yield to the Devil, go over to his Party, and
become Members of his Congregation, where all the Laughter
is not only vain and foolish, but that it is a Laughter among
Devils; that all who are there, are upon prophane Ground,
and hearing Musick in the very Porch of Hell. After he
has bestow'd all this fine Language upon it, and all these
fragrant Flowers of Rhetorick, he assures us, that the
Playhouse is all that he has said, not thro' any accidental
Abuse, as any innocent or good Thing may be abused,
but by its genuine Hellish Nature; which is directly contrary to what the foremention'd illustrious Prelate has said.
Mr. *Law* says, that every Entertainment of the Stage is
in its Nature unlawful, abominable, and infernal. The
Archbishop assures us, that the Entertainments of the
Stage may be so managed, as not only to be innocent,
but useful and instructive; nay, that they may even become necessary for the exposing some certain Follies, and
the correcting some certain Vices.

As

As Mr. *Law* has ſhewn his Want of Sincerity in the foreſaid Quotation, he gives us great Reaſons to ſuſpeᴄt it in his Invectives againſt the Drama. For 'tis hard to conceive, that a Man of Letters ſhould be ſo ignorant of the Nature of a legitimate Dramatick Poem, as thoſe Invectives ſuppoſe him; for 'tis ſuch only that we pretend to defend, and abhor the Productions of ignorant and impure Poetaſters as much as he does. 'Tis hard to conceive, that a Man who has read the Claſſicks,-ſhould not know that a legitimate Dramatick Poem, either of the Comick or Tragick Kind, is a Fable, and as much a Fable as any one of *Æſop*'s, agreeing in Genus, and differing only in Species. *Terence* has told him in almoſt every one of his Prologues, that every Comedy is a Fable; and he begins his very firſt to *Andrea* with it,

Poeta cum primum animum ad ſcribendum appulit,
Id ſibi negoti credidit ſolum dari,
Populo ut placerent quas feciſſet Fabulas.

And *Horace* tells us the ſame Thing concerning Tragedy, more than once or twice :

Neve minor quinto, neu ſit productior actu
Fabula.   **De Arte Poet.**

And we find in the ſame Treatiſe;

Interdum ſpecioſa locis, morataque recte
Fabula.

And likewiſe again ;

Nec Quodcunque volet poſcat ſibi Fabula credi.

Mr. *Law* cannot but know, that the Inſtruction by Fables and Parables, which mean the ſame Thing, was
mightily

mightily in Ufe among the wife Ancients, and efpecially among the facred Writers; that we have an Example of it, of about three thoufand Years ftanding, in the Parable of *Jothan*. And that *Jefus Chrift*, who beft knew the Nature of Men, made ufe of Fables or Parables, as moft proper at the fame Time, both to pleafe, and inftruct, and perfwade. For a Fable is a Difcourfe moft aptly contrived to form the Manners of Men by Inftructions difguifed under the Allegory of an Action. And therefore he could not chufe but know, that every legitimate Dramatick Poem, either of the Comick or Tragick Kind, is not a mere Diverfion, as he pretends, but a philofophical and moral Lecture, in which the Poet is Teacher, and the Spectators are his Difciples, as *Horace* infinuates in the three following Verfes:

Nec minimum meruere Decus veftigia Græca
Aufi deferere & celebrare Domeftica Facta
Vel qui Prætextas, vel qui docuere togatas.

And knowing all this, he could not but know that 'tis very hard, if not very extravagant, to put the frequenting moral Lectures upon the fame Foot with Idolatry.

If Mr. *Law* has read either *Ariftotle* or any of his Interpreters, as 'tis hard to imagine that he fhould think himfelf qualified to write againft the Stage if he had read none of them, he cannot but know, that as the Action of a Dramatick Fable is univerfal and allegorical, the Characters are fo likewife. For as when *Æfop* introduces a Horfe, or a Dog, or a Wolf, or a Lion, he does not pretend to fhew us any fingular Animal, but only to fhew the
Nature

[8]

Nature of that Creature, as far as the Occasion where it appears admits of; so when a Dramatick Poet sets before us his Characters, he does not pretend to entertain us with particular Persons, tho' he may give them particular Names; but proposes to lay before us general and allegorical Fantoms, and to make them talk and act as Persons compounded of such and such Qualities, would talk and act upon like Occasions, in order to give proper Instructions.

Now as a Dramatick Fable is a Discourse invented to form the Manners by Instructions disguised under the Allegory of an Action, it follows, that in a Dramatick Fable for the proving the Moral, 'tis as necessary to introduce vicious as virtuous Characters, and to make them speak and act, as all Persons compounded of their Qualities would be obliged by Nature to speak and act upon the like Occasions; as *Æsop*, for the Sake of his Morals, does not only introduce innocent and peaceable Creatures, as Horses, and Sheep, and Cows, and Dogs; but likewise noxious and violent ones, as Lions and Bears, and Wolves, and Foxes: But the Poet at the same time ought to take care that the Vices should be shewn after such a Manner, as to render them odious or ridiculous, and not agreeable or desirable; and that the Reader should reap no Pleasure from the Agreeableness of the Vices, but only from a just Imitation of Nature.

I make no Doubt, Sir, but that I have said enough to satisfie you or any of your Friends to whom you may happen to shew this Letter, that as every true Dramatick
Poem

Poem is a Fable as much as any one of *Æsop's* ; it has in its Nature a direct Tendency to teach moral Virtue, and can therefore never be contrary to a Chriſtian Temper and Spirit, which, where-ever it is, incites us to good Works, that is, to the Performance of moral Duties. But there is every Jot as much Difference between a true Dramatick Poem, and the Production of an ignorant obſcene Poe-taſter, as there is between two religious Books, the *Bible* and the *Alcoran.* Now will Mr. *Law* affirm, that becauſe the *Alcoran* is full of egregious Falſhoods, and of mon-ſtrous Fanatick Extravagancies, therefore we ought not to read the *Bible ?* It belongs to none but to an Atheiſt, or ſome other unbelieving Sceptick, to make ſuch a Con-cluſion.

Sir, As 'tis hard to conceive that Mr. *Law* ſhould be ignorant of what we have ſaid above, both concerning the ſacred Writings, and the Nature of a Dramatick Poem ; and equally hard, if he is not ignorant, to believe him a Writer of Sincerity and Integrity ; ſo it ſeems to be as hard to conceive, that a Man of his Years, and conſe-quently of his Experience, ſhould be utterly a Stranger to the preſent State of Religion, and Virtue and Vice, a-mong us ; or that, if he is not a Stranger to it, he ſhould be capable of writing ſo malicious or ſo erroneous a Trea-tiſe as that which he has lately publiſh'd againſt the Stage.

Before I come to ſpeak of the preſent State of Religion among us, I deſire Leave to tranſlate a Paſſage from *Da-cier's* Preface to his excellent Comment on *Ariſtotle's Art of Poetry.* If the Quotation appears to be of more than

C   ordinary

ordinary Length to you, I comfort my felf with this Re-
flection, that you will attend to an Author of more than
ordinary Learning and Judgment, and who can fpeak fo
much better in this Caufe than myfelf.

‘ Poetry, fays that moft judicious Critick, is an Art
‘ which was invented for the Inftruction of Mankind, and
‘ an Art which is by Confequence ufeful. ’Tis a Truth
‘ acknowledg’d by all the World, that every Art is in
‘ itfelf good, becaufe there is none whofe End and Defign
‘ is not fo: But as it is no lefs true, that Men are apt to
‘ abufe the very beft Things, and to pervert the very beft
‘ Defigns, that which was at firft invented as a wholfome
‘ Remedy, may afterwards become a very dangerous Poifon.
‘ I am obliged to declare, then, that in what I fay of
‘ Tragedy, I fpeak not of corrupted Tragedy: For ’tis
‘ not in Works that are deprav’d and vicious that we are
‘ to fearch for the Reafon and the Defign of Nature, but
‘ in thofe which are found and intire; when I fay this, I
‘ fpeak of ancient Tragedy, of that which is conform-
‘ able to the Rules of *Ariftotle*, which I dare pronounce
‘ to be the moft ufeful and moft neceffary of all Diver-
‘ fions whatever.
‘ If it were in our Power to oblige all Men to follow
‘ the Precepts which the Gofpel lays down, nothing could
‘ be more happy for Mankind. In living conformably to
‘ them, they would find true Repofe, folid Pleafure, and
‘ a fure Remedy for all their Infirmities; and they might
‘ then look upon Tragedy as a ufelefs Thing, and which
‘ would be infinitely below them. How could they look
‘ upon it in any other Light, fince the Heathens themfelves
‘ beheld

' beheld it in the very fame, as foon as they had embraced
' the Study of Philofophy. They confefs, that if People
' could be always nourifh'd with the folid Truths of Phi-
' lofophy, the Philofophers had never had Recourfe to
' Fables, in order to give them Inftruction. But as fo
' much Corruption could not bear fo much Wifdom, the
' Philofophers were obliged to look for a Remedy for the
' Diforder which they faw in Mens Pleafures; for which
' they invented Tragedy, and they offered it to the World,
' not as the moft excellent Thing of which Men could
' make their Employment and their Study, but yet as a
' Means to correct thofe Exceffes, in which they were
' wont to be plunged at their folemn Feafts; and to ren-
' der thofe Diverfions ufeful to them, which Cuftom and
' their Weaknefs had render'd neceffary, and their Cor-
' ruption very dangerous.

' What Men were formerly, they are To-day; and what
' they are To-day, they will be hereafter; they have the
' fame Paffions which they always had, and run with the
' fame Eagernefs after Pleafure. To undertake to reduce
' them in this Condition by the Severity of Precepts, is
' endeavouring to put a Bridle on a mad Horfe in the
' greateft Rapidity of his Courfe. In the mean time,
' there is no Middle; Men will fall into the moft criminal
' Exceffes, unlefs we find Pleafures for them which are
' wife and regular. 'Tis fome Degree of Happinefs, that
' a Remnant of Reafon inclines them to love fuch Diver-
' fions as are confiftent with Order, and fuch Amufe-
' ments as are not incompatible with Truth. And I am
' perfuaded, that we are obliged in Charity to make our
' Advantage of this Inclination, that we may not give

C 2   ' time

' time to Debauchery entirely to quench that Spark of
' right Reaſon which ſtill may be ſeen to glimmer in them.
' We preſcribe to diſtemper'd Perſons; and Tragedy is the
' only Remedy, from which, in their preſent-Condition,
' they can reap any Advantage; for 'tis the only Diverſion
' in which they can find the Profitable united with the
' Pleaſant.'

Thus far Monſieur *Dacier*. And here, *Sir*, I beg Leave
to obſerve, that, notwithſtanding our Reformation, we
have as few Perſons here in *England* who have the true
Spirit of Chriſtianity in them, as there are in *France* :
But there is this Difference between them and us; In
France, all own themſelves Chriſtians publickly; none of
them dare renounce the Name, tho' few of them are the
Thing : But among us, How many open Diſſenters are
there from Chriſtianity itſelf? How many Atheiſts? How
many Deiſts? How many Free-thinkers of a Thouſand
Kinds? who all of them refuſe to join in our ſacred Rites;
ſome of them, as the Atheiſts, believing them to be ſenſe-
leſs and ridiculous; and others, as the Deiſts, eſteeming
them to be blaſphemous and idolatrous. Then what
School of publick Virtue and of publick Spirit have we
for too great a Part of our Youth, but our Theatres
only?

'Tis very ſtrange that Mr. *Law* ſhould be ſo ignorant
of the preſent State of Religion among us, as not to fore-
ſee that the wild Enthuſiaſm, and the ſpiritual Fanatical
Rant, which abounds ſo much in his late Pamphlet, would
afford Matter of Scorn and Laughter to Infidels and Free-
thinkers

thinkers of all Sorts, and render our moſt ſacred Religion
ſtill more contemptible among them.

When Mr. *Law* ſays, in the 16th Page of his Pamphlet,
that *It cannot be doubted by any one, that the Playhouſe is
a Nurſery of Vice and Debauchery, and that the Effect it
has upon Peoples Manners is as viſible as the Sun at Noon*;
he ſeems to know as little of the preſent State of Vice
among us, as he pretends to do of Religion. The preſent reigning Vices of the Town, are Drinking, Gaming,
Curſing, Swearing, Prophaneſs, Corruption of all Sorts,
as Bribing, Tricking, Oppreſſion, Cheating, Whoring and
execrable Sodomy. And Mr. *Law*, forſooth, has the Face
to tell the World, that the Playhouſe encourages all theſe;
that it is the Sink of Corruption and Debauchery; and
that that is not the State of it thro' any accidental Abuſe,
but that Corruption and Debauchery are the truly natural
and genuine Effects of the Stage-Entertainment, that is,
of any Stage-Entertainment. Now to ſhew the Folly and
the Arrogance of theſe Aſſertions, let us conſider theſe
Vices one by one.

Firſt then; Does the Theatre encourage Drunkenneſs?
No; it neither does nor can encourage it: To ſhew it,
is enough to render it odious or ridiculous. To ſhew a
Man drunk, is to ſhew a Fool or a Madman, in whom
the Creator's Image is for a Time intirely defaced, and
who, while he continues in that State, ſtands in need of a
Guardian. Beſides, nothing is more certain, than that
brutal Vice rages moſt in the Scum and Off-ſcowring of
the People, who neither have nor ever had the leaſt Communication

munication with the Playhouſe. 'Tis true, Men of Thought may be ſometimes drawn into it, but they naturally hate it ; for Drunkenneſs is a mortal Enemy to Thought, and conſequently Thought to that.

Does the Playhouſe encourage Gaming? So far from that, that Gaming has increaſed ten-fold, ſince *Collier's* Books againſt the Stage were publiſhed ; and ſince when, whole Plays have been writ to ſhew it dangerous and deſtructive, to ſhew the unſpeakable Harm it does to both Sexes, and particularly to the Women ; *to ſhew that Gaming, by giving Men a Privilege of being familiar with, and ſometimes rude to Women, removes that Awe which Nature has placed between the Sexes, as the ſtrongeſt Bulwark of Chaſtity ; that when a young Lady, even of the ſtricteſt, the moſt unblemiſh'd Honour, loſes a Sum of Money, which ſhe dares not own to her Relations, and which ſhe cannot pay without them, and loſes it to an agreeable young Fellow, who perhaps loves her, and has a ſecret Deſign upon her, ſhe finds a Temptation that trys her utmoſt Virtue.*

Does the Playhouſe encourage Swearing and Curſing ? Both Reaſon and Experience aſſure us that it does not. They who walk the Streets in the Weſt End of the Town may be ſufficiently convinced, that it rages moſt in the Lees of the People, who never knew what a Playhouſe was. It infects even their Wives and their Children, as it very rarely does thoſe of the better Sort. As common Swearing is a fooliſh brutal Vice, that brings neither Pleaſure nor Profit with it, and is the Reſult of want of Thought ; it follows, that the fooliſh brutal Part of the People muſt be

moſt

moſt infeſted with it. Of the Women that frequent the Playhouſe, few are addiſted to it but the common Strumpets ; and of the Men, none but Bullies, Rakes, and giddy Coxcombs. If a Comick Poet draws any of theſe, in order to correſt and amend them, he is obliged to ſhew them ſometimes Swearing, or he leaves out one of their Charaſteriſticks. But he cannot fail of ſhewing that very Quality either odious or ridiculous, when it appears in Perſons who are themſelves both the one and the other. And if he ſhews it either odious or ridiculous, that ſurely will invite none of the Audience to imitate it.

We equally deny, that the Playhouſe encourages any other Sort of Prophaneſs. But as a Play is a Fable, that is, a Compoſition of Truth and Fiſtion (as we have obſerved above;) as the Aſtion is feigned and the Moral true ; as Charaſters are neceſſary for the carrying on the Aſtion, and for proving the Moral, and vicious Charaſters as neceſſary, and perhaps ſometimes more neceſſary, than are the good ones ; as to ſhew vicious Charaſters, and to expoſe them, 'tis abſolutely neceſſary to put vicious Sentiments into their Mouths, it follows, that the moſt criminal Sentiments, and the moſt violent Paſſions, are allowable in vicious and violent Charaſters ; the moſt ungovern'd Fury, and the moſt outragious Blaſphemy itſelf, not excepted ; provided they are adapted to the Charaſter and the Occaſion, and the Charaſter and the Occaſion are neceſſary for the Moral. *Virgil* has every where ſhewn *Mezentius* a Contemner of the Gods, and a Blaſphemer of them ; yet we never heard that the moſt bigotted of his Cotemporaries ever accuſed *Virgil* upon that Account. *Milton*, in the ſecond Book of
Paradice

Paradice loſt, makes the Devils, in their infernal Council, blaſpheme in a moſt outragious Manner; and yet, as they ſpeak agreeably to their Characters and the Occaſion, no Man has ever been ſo weak or ſo unjuſt, as to accuſe *Milton* for that Blaſphemy, or to give all his Readers to the Devil for being entertained with it. On the contrary, all Men of good Underſtanding, and good Taſte, have been peculiarly charm'd with that very Book, as one of the moſt beautiful of that admirable Poem. *Cowley* makes not only the Devil, but *Goliah* blaſpheme;

> *Thus he blaſphem'd aloud; The Hills around,*
> *Flatt'ring his Voice, reſtor'd the dreadful Sound.*

and yet has been never blamed for it. The Book of *Job* is canonical, and is firmly believed to have been writ by divine Inſpiration. Tho' it is full of uncharitable Judgments, and is not free from Blaſphemy, yet the Inſtructions which that divine Parable or Fable gives, proceed in a great meaſure from that very Blaſphemy, and thoſe uncharitable Judgments. But now, if a Poet is allow'd to put Blaſphemy into the Mouth of one of his Characters, provided he takes care to puniſh him for it, he is certainly at Liberty to do the like by any inferior Prophaneſs.

The Three Nonjuring Prieſts who have attack'd the Stage, have made ſuch a Noiſe about nothing as Prophaneſs; it ſometimes drops three or four Times in one Page from their tautologous Pens; and they have chiefly accuſed our Comedies for it: The Unreaſonableneſs of which may appear from hence, that all our true Comedies are but Copies of the fooliſh or vicious Originals of the Age.

Age. Certainly never Man knew what a Comedy was better than did *Moliere.* Now when in the Critic of the *Ecole des Femmes,* he is endeavouring to prove, by the Mouth of *Dorante,* that Comedy is harder to write than Tragedy, he gives the following Reafon for it: *Lors que vous peignez des Heros, vous faites ce que vous voulez; ce font des Portraits a plaifir, ou l'ou ne cherche de reffem-blance; et vous n' avez qu'a fuivre les Traits d'une Ima-gination qui fe donne l'effor, et qui fouvent laiffe le vrai pour atraper le* Merveilleux. *Mais lors que vous peignez les Hom-mes, il faut peindre d' apres Nature; on veut qui ces Portraits reffemblent, et vous n'avez rien fait fi vous n'y faites recon-noitre le Gens de votre Siecle.* That is to fay; When you draw Heroes, you are at your own Liberty; thofe are Pictures at the Painter's Pleafure, in which no Body looks for Likenefs; and you have nothing to do but to indulge the Flight of a foaring Imagination. But when you paint Men, you muft draw after Nature; the World expects that thofe Pictures fhould be like; and you have done nothing at all, unlefs you fhew your Readers or your Spectators the People of the Age you live in.

Now with Regard to Prophanefs, our Comedies are the fainteft Copies in the World, and you may often hear more Prophanefs in one Night's Converfation at a Tavern or an Eating-houfe, than you fhall hear from the Stage in a Year. For Atheifts, Deifts, Arians, and Socinians, are wont to fay at their private Meetings, what no one dares to pronounce on the Stage. Now are not thefe Nonjuring Priefts either very wife, or very confcientious Perfons? Our Comedies are but Copies of the foolifh and vicious Origi-

D   nals

nals of the Age ; and 'tis the Bufinefs of the Copies to expofe, and fatyrize, and ridicule thofe foolifh and thofe vicious Originals. Now thefe Nonjuring Priefts having nothing to fay againft thofe foolifh and thofe vicious Originals, which moft certainly corrupt and debauch the Age, make it their Bufinefs to fall foul on the Copies, which chaftife, and fatyrize, and ridicule the Originals.

What I have faid of the Stage with Relation to Prophanefs, is in Proportion true, with Regard to all other Vices. Now fince our Comedies are but Copies of the foolifh and the vicious Originals of the Age in which we live, and Copies which do by no means come up to the Originals, I appeal to all the World, if it does not unanfwerably follow from what I have faid, that the Originals of the Age debauch the Stage, by which latter, the Age never poffibly can be debauched. The Stage was eftablifh'd in *England* towards the Beginning of Queen *Elizabeth's* Reign ; whereas the Manners of the People continued generally found till beyond the Middle of the laft Century And the Manners of the People continuing generally found, the Stage remain'd generally chafte : But at the Reftoration of *Charles* the Second, the Court returning from abroad, corrupted by foreign Luxury, quickly debauch'd the Town ; and the Court and the Town jointly endeavour'd to debauch the Stage, becaufe our Comick Poets were obliged to copy their lewd Originals, in order to expofe and reform them.

As for Corruption of any Sort, whether it be Tricking, Oppreffing, Bribing, Sharping, Cheating, the true Poet, who

who is perfectly free from all Avarice, is leaft of all ad-
dicted to it.

——————————— *Vatis Avarus.*

Non temere eft animus, verfus amat, hoc ftudet unum
Detrimenta, fugas fervorum, incendia ridet ;
Non fraudem focio, puerove incogitat ullam
Pupillo ;   Horace Epift. ad Auguftum.

Their ufual Poverty is a fignal Proof of this : For as the
Love of Money is the Source of all Corruption, he who
defpifes Gold, is above all the Vices that attend it. And
Poverty attended with great Parts, may very well pafs for
a pretty fure Sign of Honefty. A Dramatick Poet therefore being averfe from all Corruption himfelf, if ever he
defcribes any Kind of it, is fure to make it both odious
and ridiculous.

I come now to almoft the only Charge againft the Stage
which feems to have any thing of real Weight in it, and
that is, That it excites in Mens Minds the natural Love
of Women. And here by this Charge may be meant two
Things ; the one is, That it excites in Men a Defire to
the unlawful Enjoyment of Women ; the other is, That it
inclines them to that violent Paffion of Love, which is
fometimes between the two Sexes.

As to the firft Part of the Charge, that it excites in
Men a Defire to the unlawful Enjoyment of Women ; if
there are any Paffages in our Plays that are chargeable
with that Guilt, or that defile the Imaginations of an Audience with unchaft and immodeft Images, they are nei-

ther

ther natural to the Drama nor neceſſary, but flagrant A-
buſes of it, and contrary to the very Deſign of the Art;
and thoſe Paſſages ought to be baniſh'd from the Stage for
ever. And yet I cannot help thinking, that if ever thoſe
Paſſages could be excuſable, they would be ſo at this Jun-
cture, when the execrable Sin of Sodomy is ſpread ſo
wide, that the foreſaid Paſſages might be of ſome Uſe to
the reducing Mens Minds to the natural Deſire of Women. Let Fornication be ever ſo crying a Sin, yet Sodomy is a Crime of a thouſand times a deeper Dye. A
Crime that forc'd down ſupernatural Fire from Heaven, to
extinguiſh its infernal Flames; a Crime that would have
obliged even righteous *Lot* to proſtitute his two chaſt and
virgin Daughters, in order to prevent it. I cannot here omit
obſerving one Thing, That this unnatural Sin has very
much increaſed ſince *Collier's* Books were publiſh'd againſt
the Stage. There were no leſs than four Perſons condemned for it the laſt Seſſions; and I am inform'd, that
ſeveral more have been ſince apprehended for it : The like
of which was never heard of in *Great Britain* before.

As for the Paſſion of Love, by which the Hearts of
Men and Women are ſometimes mutually and violently inclined to each other ; if the Paſſion is kept within the
Bounds of Nature, if the Object and the Intention of it
is lawful, or if 'tis puniſh'd when 'tis unlawful, I am of
the Opinion, that it cannot have the leaſt ill Conſequence;
'tis certainly a Check upon wandring looſe Deſires; it gives a
very great and very harmleſs Pleaſure, and has a direct Tendency to the keeping the two Sexes ſtedfaſt and firm to the
natural Love of each other : For not only the Affections of
the

the Men have wildly wander'd from Nature, as is manifeſt to all the World, but not a few of the Women too
have endeavour'd to make themſelves the Center of their
own Happineſs. St. *Paul* is pleas'd to reprove this unnatural Affection of the *Roman* Dames in the firſt Chapter
of his Epiſtle to the *Romans*. And Mr. *Law* is deſired to
take Notice, that he lays thoſe unnatural Deſires not upon
their going to Plays, but upon their Idolatry ; Verſe 22,
Profeſſing themſelves to be wiſe, they became Fools. Verſe
*23, And changed the Glory of the incorruptible God into an
Image made like to corruptible Man, and to Birds, and four-
footed Beaſts, and creeping Things.* Verſe 24, *Wherefore
God alſo gave them up to Uncleanneſs, to diſhonour their own
Bodies between themſelves.* Verſe 25, *Who changed the
Truth of God into a Lie, and worſhipped and ſerved the
Creature rather than the Creator, who is bleſſed for ever.
Amen.* Verſe 26, *For this Cauſe God gave them up to vile
Affections : For even their Women did change the natural
Uſe into that which is againſt Nature.* Verſe 27, *And likewiſe the Men, leaving the natural Uſe of the Women, burned
in their own Luſts one toward another, Men with Men working that which is unſeemly, and receiving in themſelves that
Recompence of their Errors which was meet.* And Mr. *Law*
may be pleaſed to obſerve, that the Apoſtle here gives us
another ſignal Proof, that he does not put Idolatry and
going to Plays upon an equal Foot. And here, *Sir,* I deſire Leave to make another Remark, and that is, That of
all the Countries of the Chriſtian World, that Country has
been, is, and is like to be, the moſt infamous for this execrable Vice, in which Idolatry has ſet up its Head Quar-
ters.

Sir,

Sir, You are very well acquainted with the exact Judgment of the late *French* Satyrift, who was an Honour to *France.* That he was very far from being a Friend to the Corruption of the Stage, will appear from the following Paffage of the fourth Canto of his *Art of Poetry* ; where he is giving his Advice to the Poets who were his Cotemporaries.

Que votre ame & vos mœurs peints dans tous vos ouvrages
N' offrent jamais de vous que de nobles Images.
Je ne puis eftimer ces dangereux Auteurs,
Qui de l' honneur en vers infames deferteurs,
Trahiffant la vertu fur un papier coupable,
Aux yeux de leurs Lectures rendent le vice aimable.

Tho' I know very well, that no one underftands this Author better than you do ; yet as this Letter is to pafs thro' your Hand to the Prefs, I defire Leave to tranflate the Paffage, for the Benefit of thofe who are not ufed to *French.*

Let your Soul and your Manners, appearing in your Works
to your Readers, never offer any but noble Ideas of you.
I can have no Efteem for thofe dangerous Authors, thofe in-
famous Deferters of Honour in their Verfes, who being Tray-
tors to Virtue in their guilty Lines, render Vice lovely to the
Eyes of thofe who perufe them.

And yet immediately after comes his Approbation of Love in Dramatick Poems:

Je ne fuis pas pourtant de ces triftes Efprits
Qui banniffant l'Amour de tous chaftes ècrits,
D' un fi riche ornement veulent priver la Scene :
Traitent d' empoifonneurs & Rodrigue & Chimene.

L' amour

L' amour le moins honneste exprimé chastement,
N' excite point en nous de honteux movement.
Didon a beau gemir & m' étaler ses charmes ;
Je condamne sa faute, en partageant ses larmes.

And yet, fays he, *I am none of those splenetick Souls,*
who banishing Love from all chaste Composures, endeavour to
deprive the Stage of so rich an Ornament. The most disho-
nourable Love, if 'tis chastly express'd, excites no shameful
Motion in us. In vain does Dido *lament and groan, exposing*
all her Charms to me ; I condemn her Conduct at the very
Time that I partake of her Grief.

I now return to the Charge of Hypocrify ; for which
there are very just Grounds of Suspicion from the Stile
and Language of this Pamphlet. For is not this little
Treatife, which is pretended to be writ thro' a Zeal for
the Christian Religion, writ in downright Antichristian Language ? Is this Pamplet writ in the Language of Modesty,
of Humility, of Meeknefs ? Is it writ in the attractive
Language of Charity ? On the contrary, Does not Mr.
Law feem to have taken all his Degrees at a certain Uni-
verfity between the Bridge and the Tower ? And as the
Difciples of our Saviour, from Dealers in Fifh became the
Apoftles of their Mafter ; this falfe Apoftle feems to fet
up for Water Doctor, and from a Prieft to become a Dealer
in Fifh. For he has not only the Tropes, and the Figures,
and all the Rhetorical Flowers, but the very Tautologies
of those obftreperous Dealers in quiet and mute Animals.
For the forefaid obftreperous Dealers, are not contented
with calling Rogue, or Whore, or Bitch, or Villain, once,

they

they will repeat it fifty Times; and their Fellow-Collegiate who difputes with them, will return it fifty-fold.

I defire that you would give me leave to prefent you with fome of Mr. *Law*'s Rhetorical Flowers.

At the Bottom of the fecond Page of his Pamphlet, he tells us, That there is more to be faid in Behalf of Popery than of going to Plays. For that is plainly his Meaning, tho' he difguifes it by the Terms that he ufes. And towards the Top of the third Page, he is no lefs pofitive, that God is lefs difpleafed with Popery than he is with going to Plays. It looks as if Mr. *Law* would be very glad to exchange Plays for Popery.

In all the reft of the fecond Page, he puts them upon an equal Foot; and affures us, that the Entertainment of the Stage is contrary to more Doctrines of Scripture than the Worfhip of Images.

What, tho' we grant it; Intemperance in Eating, Drinking, and Venery, is contrary to more Doctrines of Scripture, than is either Murder, or High-Treafon; and yet either Murder or High-Treafon fingly, is ten Times a greater Sin than all the forementioned Three together. Sometimes he is making Idolatry, that is Popery, lefs criminal than going to Plays: Sometimes he is for making them equal, and endeavouring to revive the old ftoical Opinion, *Omnia peccata funt æqualia*; All Sins are equal: A Paradox that would tend to make Chriftianity as ridiculous, as it help'd to do *Pagan* Stoicifm.

In

In the firſt Paragraph of the 4th Page. *You go to hear Plays you ſay — I tell you*, ſays Mr. *Law, you go to hear Ribaldry and Prophaneſs; that you entertain your Mind with extravagant Thoughts, wild Rant, blaſphemous Speeches, wanton Amours, prophane Jeſts, and impure Paſſions.* [Ay, now the Language of the College begins.] And a little lower, *He who goes to a Play, diverts himſelf with the Lewdneſs, Impudence, Prophaneſs, and impure Diſcourſes of the Stage.* And a little lower, in the ſame Page, *This is plainly the Caſe of the Stage; it is an Entertainment that conſiſts of lewd, impudent, prophane Diſcourſes.* And Pag. 7, *It is an Entertainment made up of Lewdneſs, Prophaneſs, and all the extravagant Rant of diſorder'd Paſſions.* At the Top of Page 8. he is endeavouring once more to make Popery leſs ſinful than going to Plays; and by the ſame Piece of ſpiritual Sophiſtry, he confirms this religious Lie; becauſe, forſooth, the Stage, with its *lewd prophane Diſcourſes*, offends againſt more Doctrines of plain Scripture than Popery: Which is proving one groſs Piece of Falſhood, by another that is much greater.

About the Middle of the ſame Page, he brings an Argument againſt the Stage from the Iniquity of the Players, againſt whom he inveighs with his uſual Sophiſtry and Uncharitableneſs: Which is full as wiſe and as juſt, as it would be to bring an Argument againſt the Church, from the Vices of ſome ſpiritual Comedians. *The Players are Men and Women*, ſays he, *equally bold, in all Inſtances of Prophaneſs, Paſſion, and Immodeſty;* whoſe Buſineſs, Pag. 9, *is prophane, wicked, lewd, and immodeſt;* and a little lower in the ſame Page, *whoſe Employment is leſs Chriſtian than that of Robbers.*

For

For he muſt know very little of the Nature of Religion, ſays Mr. *Law, who can look upon Luſt, Prophaneſs, and diſor-der'd Paſſions, to be leſs contrary to Religion, than the taking Money from the right Owner.* Which is directly contrary to common Senſe and to common Utility.

Queis paria eſſe fere placuit peccata, laborant,
Cum ventum ad verum eſt : ſenſus moreſque repugnant.
Atque ipſa utilitas juſti prope mater & æqui. Hor.

Page 10, He ſpeaks of *the Blaſphemy, Prophaneſs, Lewd-neſs, Immodeſty, and wicked Rant of Plays.* And a little lower in the ſame Page, he mentions *a Collection of all the wicked, prophane, blaſphemous, lewd, impudent, deteſt-able Things that are ſaid in the Playhouſe.* And Page 11, he ſpeaks of the Entertainment of the Stage, *as it conſiſts of Love-Intrigues, blaſphemous Paſſions, prophane Diſ-courſes, lewd Deſcriptions, filthy Jeſts, and all the moſt ex-travagant Rant of wanton profligate Perſons of both Sexes ; heating and inflaming one another with all the Wantonneſs of Addreſs, the Immodeſty of Motion, and the Lewdneſs of Thought, that Wit can invent.*

And here I deſire Leave to ſay a Word, by the way, in Defence of Players, whoſe Profeſſion he very wiſely, hu-manely, and Chriſtianly, makes as unlawful as that of Robbers. Is he to be told at this Time of Day, that the Players ſay nothing of Themſelves ? They only ſpeak what the Poet puts into the Mouths of his univerſal allegorical Fantoms ; which Fantoms the Players repreſent. Can this poor Gentleman be ſo ſimple as to believe, that *Reynard, Bruin, Iſgrim,* and *Grimalkin,* ſay really of themſelves the

Things

Things that *Æsop* puts into their Mouths? The Players are only the Poet's Instruments, by which he carries on his Action, and proves his Moral. If any Musician sings a treasonable Song, and plays to it at the same time, he ought to suffer for his Crime; but would you indict the Fiddle or the Flute upon which the Tune is play'd?

What Turn Mr. *Law* design'd to serve, by being so profuse of so much fine Language he best can tell, tho' we perhaps may guess. But he could never possibly think of making Poets, or Players, or Spectators, good Christians, by railing at them for an Hour together, and treating them worse than the great Archangel dared to treat the Devil, *who durst not bring against him a railing Accusation, but only said, The Lord rebuke thee.* If he design'd to convert People by such a Proceeding, he might as well pretend to begin a Friendship with another by abusing him, and throwing Dirt at him.

But to make some Amends for treating his Fellow-Creatures with so much Antichristian Language, he uses the Devil with a great deal of Respect and Civility. For besides the gentle Terms in which he speaks of him; of his Honour, of his Glory, of his Joy, his Delight, his Pleasure, his peculiar Pleasure; as if Damnation were an honourable and a happy State; besides this, I say, he is pleased, out of his great Bounty, to settle upon him and his, to have and to hold for ever, the Freehold and Fee-Simple of all our Theatres. *One may, with the same Assurance, affirm,* says he, *that the Playhouse, not only when some prophane Play is on the Stage, but in its daily common*

E 2

Enter-

Entertainments, is as certainly the House of the Devil, as the Church is the House of God, Page 12. And a little lower in the same Page, *The Manner and Matter of Stage-Entertainments, is as undeniable a 'Proof, and as obvious to common Sense, that the House belongs to the Devil, and is the Place of his Honour, as the Matter and Manner of Church-Service prove that the Place is appropriated to God.*

Now my opinion is, That if the Devil should once become the Head-Landlord of our Theatres, he would immediately turn them into so many *Jacobite* Conventicles: For those are properly his Houses, those are properly his Temples. For the Sins which the Theatres are accused by Mr. *Law* of encouraging, are not the Devil's Sins, but our own, the Sins of Men and Women. The Devil neither drinks nor whores, nor games, nor rants, nor gormandizes. But the Sins which are carried on in a *Jacobite* Conventicle, are the Devil's own Sins; his two great original Sins, Lying and Rebellion. There all those false Doctrines are carried on, of Hereditary Right, Divine Right, Indefeasible Right, Absolute Power, Uncontroulable Power, Passive Obedience, Unconditional Obedience; Doctrines invented on purpose to make and flatter Tyrants, who are the Devil's Viceroys. *For as good Kings are God's Vicegerents, sure a Tyrant is Hell's Viceroy.* The Place where the Pretender's Cause is carried on, is properly the Temple of the Devil, the original Pretender.

When Mr. *Law* affirms, That the Playhouse is the Sink of Corruption and Debauchery, Page 15, and that this is not the State of it, thro' any accidental Abuse, as any innocent

nocent or good Thing may be abufed, but that Corruption and Debauchery are the truly natural and genuine Effects of the Stage Entertainments; is it poffible that he can be fo ignorant as he pretends to make himfelf? Can he be ignorant, that by affirming this, he contradicts what has been the common Senfe of Mankind for two thoufand Years; and that he contradicts the Opinions and the Judgments of the greateft, and wifeft, and moft virtuous Men, of the greateft, and wifeft, and moft virtuous Nations, during that vaft Space of Time? If Corruption and Debauchery were the natural and genuine Effects of Theatrical Entertainments; would they have been encouraged by the great Legiflators, the moft learned Philofophers, and the wifeft Rulers of the freeft States in the World?

No Body knows better than Mr. *Law*, that of all publick Diverfions, the Drama is the moft reafonable, manly, noble, and inftructive Diverfion; the excelling in which, fhews the Excellence and the Strength of Genius of that particular Nation where it appears, and by that Means advances its Reputation with other Nations, and augments its Power; and that therefore Dramatick Performances have been fo cherifhed and efteemed by the wifeft Rulers of the nobleft Nations, that they have been maintain'd by the publick Treafure; and the Magiftrate has not thought it at all below him, to have the Regulation and the immediate Infpection of it : Which is an undeniable Proof, that they did not at all miftruft that it was natural to thofe Entertainments to corrupt and debauch their People.

The

The Drama is in itfelf fo excellent, and to excel in it requires fo many great Qualities, that of all the Nations we hear of among the Ancients, but Two were capable of proper conftant Theatrical Entertainments; and thofe Two were the wifeft, braveft, and moft virtuous of all the Nations; fo famous for their great Actions in War, and fo illuftrious for the Arts of Peace, that to know what they were, is become a principal Part of the Learning of us Moderns; and 'tis accounted fcandalous in a Gentleman to be ignorant of what they faid, and wrote, and did; and yet to know what their Tragick and Comick Poets were, and what they wrote, is none of the meaneft Branches of that very Learning.

What Opinion the *Grecians* themfelves had of their Drama; how far they believed their Tragick Poets able to infpire their Countrymen with the Love of their Country, with the Love of Liberty, of Virtue, and of true Glory, and with a magnanimous Contempt of Death for the publick Good; may be gathered from the unanimous Confent of *Greece*, and particularly from the Honours done by the *Athenians* to their Tragick Poets, who made them Governors of Provinces, Generals of their Armies, and Guardians of the publick Liberty. For when the *Athenians* fettled a greater Fund for the fupporting the Magnificence of their Tragick Reprefentations, than for the Maintenance of their Fleets and Armies, we may juftly conclude that it was their Opinion, that their Tragick Poets, by conftantly fetting before them the Calamities of Tyrants, defended them from far more dangerous Enemies than thofe which their Armies were fent to encounter, and that was from
their

their own afpiring Citizens. As no People were ever more jealous of their Liberties than the *Athenians*, none ever knew better that Corruption and Debauchery are inconfiftent with Liberty; and therefore it never in the leaft enter'd into the Thoughts of that great People, that Corruption and Debauchery were the natural Effects of Dramatick Entertainments.

Nor can it be objected with any manner of Juftice, that it was the Fury of the *Athenian* Populace, running mad after their Pleafures, that made them fo warmly efpoufe the Drama. The greateft and the wifeft Philofophers of that renown'd Republick declared moft warmly and moft loudly for it. *Ariftotle* writ an admirable Syftem of Rules for the compofing Dramatick Poems, with that Right Hand that has given us fo many excellent Leffons of Morality. And *Socrates*, the wifeft and the moft virtuous of all the Philofophers, who made it the whole Bufinefs of his Life to inftruct his Countrymen in moral Virtue, did not think it in the leaft below his Wifdom and his Virtue, to affift *Euripides* in the writing his Tragedies.

That the *Romans* did not yield to the *Grecians* in the Efteem which they had for Dramatick Entertainments, and the Belief that they were capable of contributing to the Glory and the Felicity of a mighty State, and to the Glory and Felicity of the Authors of them, we may gather from the Actions of their wifeft Statefmen, their greateft Captains, and their fevereft Philofophers. Their greateft Captains and their wifeft Statefmen not only encouraged Dramatick Poems, but vouchfafed to write them themfelves.

felves. *Scipio*, the wife, the virtuous *Scipio*, writ Comedy with that conquering Hand that won the Empire of the
World at *Zama*. *Auguftus Cæfar*, as famous for the Arts
of Peace as his Succefs in War, renown'd for the wholfome
Laws he enacted, and for his reforming the Manners of
the People, begun the Tragedy of *Ajax*, tho' he could not
finifh it ; but found it eafier to make himfelf Emperor of
the World, than a great Dramatick Poet. *Cicero*, the Cham-
pion of the *Roman* Liberties, in twenty Places of his Phi-
lofophick Treatifes, quotes the *Roman* Tragick Poets.
And *Seneca*, who thro' the Opinion which *Agrippina* had
of the Strictnefs and the Severity of his Virtue, was in-
trufted with the Education of a Prince, upon whofe Conduct the Happinefs of Mankind depended ; *Seneca*, who,
by fo many admirable Leffons of moral Virtue, has obliged
all the Lovers of Wit and Virtue for ever, did not think
writing Tragedy an Employment at all below him.

Now, *Sir*, I appeal to you, whether it does not logi-
cally and neceffarily follow, from what has been faid,
that either Mr. *Law* muft believe, that the Great Men a-
mong the ancient *Grecians* and *Romans*, their Captains,
Statefmen, and Philofophers, wanted common Senfe ; or he
cannot poffibly believe, that Corruption and Debauchery
are the natural Effects of Theatrical Entertainments ; and
confequently muft be guilty of very vile Hypocrify.

There remains another ftrong Prefumption of Hypocrify
againft Mr. *Law*. For what is Mr. *Law* ? And what are
his two Predeceffors, *Collier* and *Bedford*, who attack'd the
Stage before him ? Why *Jacabite* Nonjuring Parfons all
three

three of them, who have difown'd our Eftablifh'd Church, and difown'd our Government. How come they to take up this great Concern for our Salvation in a Matter about which all our Paftors, who have the immediate Care of our Souls, are filent? Have they more Capacity to fee the enormous Crimes of Theaters, and the pretended fatal Confequences of them, than fo many great and good Men, who have been the exalted Lights of the Church fince the Reftoration? No, all the World knows, that there is not the leaft Pretence for it, nor the leaft Comparifon. Have they more true Zeal and Concern for the Chriftian Religion? No, that, as we obferved above, is inconfiftent with their Manner of treating us. The Language of *Billingfgate* can never be the Language of Charity, nor confequently of Chriftianity. Truth has not the impetuous ftormy Air which Mr. *Law* affumes, but comes in the foft and ftill Voice, like the God who infpires it; and Truth detefts and abominates the Equivocating and Prevaricating of Mr. *Collier* and Mr. *Bedford.*

But now let us confider the Time that thefe People have chofe to exert their pretended Zeal. It has been always when fomething has been about to be done, which it was thought might prove favourable to the *Pretender.* Mr. *Collier* publifh'd his *Short View* when *France* declar'd for the *Chevalier*, upon the Death of *James* II. and his *Diffuafive*, upon the great Storm, when the great Devaftation which that Huricane wrought, had amaz'd and aftonifh'd the Minds of Men, and made them obnoxious to melancholly and defponding Thoughts. I formerly expos'd the egregious hypocritical Folly of making that Storm a Divine

F   Judgment

Judgment upon the Nation for the Enormities of our Theatres. Mr. *Law* has taken the Opportunity to attack the Stage, upon the great Preparations which he heard were making abroad, and which the *Jacobites* flatter'd themſelves were deſign'd in their Favour. As for Mr. *Bedford's Serious Remonſtrance*, tho' I know nothing of the Time of publiſhing it, yet I dare to lay Odds it was either upon the Duke *D' Aumont's* being at *Somerſet-Houſe*, or upon the late Rebellion. Now all theſe Attacks upon the Stage have been Attacks upon the Government, and thoſe three worthy Perſons ſeem to me to have been at the Beck of ſome certain Superiors, and always ready at their Command to divert the People of *Great Britain* from their real Danger, by giving them Alarms in a wrong Place.

F I N I S.

ERRATA, P. 3. laſt Line but one, a ; after Experience.

of Truth, and by the Love of my Country. In the former Three, I might appear to be maintaining my own Interests. But I have, since the publishing them, been used with such extreme Ingratitude by the present Managers of the Playhouse, that I have this Ten Years been obliged, by the most barbarous Treatment, to take Leave of the Playhouse for ever.

I am, SIR,

Your most Obedient, and

most Humble Servant,

JOHN DENNIS.

The

Cabal. For 'tis in Poetry as 'tis in Politicks, Things go quite wrong

> *When Merit pines, while Clamour is prefer'd,*
> *And long Attachment waits among the Herd;*
> *When no Diſtinction where Diſtinction's due,*
> *Marks from the Many the ſuperior Few.*

A Cabal to eſpouſe a Coxcomb, may get him Money, but at the ſame Time it will procure him Infamy. Writers who have Genius will leave the Stage with the utmoſt Indignation, and every Man who underſtands it will have it in Contempt.

> *The Men who contradict the publick Voice,*
> *And ſtrive to dignify a worthleſs Choice;*
> *Attempt a Task that on that Choice reflects,*
> *And lend us Light to point out new Defects.*
> *One worthleſs Man, that gains what he pretends,*
> *Diſguſts a Thouſand unpretending Friends.*

And therefore every Writer who pretends to ſucceed by Cabals, ought to be baniſhed from every Theatre. But to ſhew the Judgment or the Integrity of our Managers of the Stage; they have for ſeveral Years paſt rejected every Play that has not had a Cabal to ſupport it.

And now, *Sir*, tho I am ſenſible that I have already detain'd you a great deal too long, for which I humbly and heartily beg your Pardon; yet, before I take Leave of you, I cannot help acquainting you, that this is the fourth Time that I have appear'd in Defence of the Stage, and in this fourth Defence I have no manner of Intereſt, but that it has been purely extorted from me by the Force

of

has been writ with more Spirit and more Grace than ordinary, has come, for the moft Part, from Volunteers.

Sir, with Submiffion to your better Judgment, there is but one Way of reviving the expiring Drama, of reftoring its original Innocence, and of augmenting its ancient Luftre, and that is by eftablifhing two annual Prizes of two hundred Pound each ; the one for Comedy, the other for Tragedy, to be given, befides the ordinary Profits of the Theatre, to him who performs beft in each of them, which is to be decided by Judges appointed on purpofe, and fworn to determine impartially; with this Provifo, that no Play fhall be received, that fhall be judged to be ever fo little offenfive to good Manners; and that every Play fhall be rejected, whofe Author can be proved to have taken the leaft Step towards the forming a Cabal ; which Defign I humbly conceive is in your Power to reduce to Practice, if you would vouchfafe to recommend it to the Government, or to a Number of Gentlemen who may be every way qualify'd to engage in fo good a Caufe.

Several Caufes may be affigned of the Decay of Dramatick Peotry, as the *Italian Opera*, which never was eftablifhed in any Country, but it immediately debafed the Poetry of that Nation: The Strangers who have been introduced among us, by feveral great Events, as the *Revolution*, the *Union*, the *Hanover Succeffion*, who not underftanding our Language, have been very inftrumental in introducing Sound and Show; the new Gentry that has ftarted up among us, fome by the Fortune of War, and fome by the Fortune of *Exchange-Alley*, who are fond of their old Entertainments of *Jack-Pudding*; but yet none of thefe has done half the Harm that has been done by Cabal.

than the Dramatick, had, by Reaſon of the Lowneſs of their Fortunes, been uncapable of exerting their Genius's in thoſe other Kinds, if they had not been firſt encouraged, and raiſed, and ſupported by the Stage. And 'tis very natural to conceive, that ſeveral others, who at the ſame time that they had large Revenues, were qualified both by Nature and Art to excel in the other Kinds, were rouzed and excited to try their Fortunes in them, by the animating Applauſes which they ſaw that our Dramatick Poets received from their raviſh'd Audiences. The Sentiment of *Virgil* might, on ſuch Occaſions, very naturally preſent itſelf to their Minds.

—— *Tentanda via eſt qua me quoque poſſim*
Tollere humo, victorque virûm volitare per ora.

And now, *Sir*, ſince the chief Encouragement not only of Plays, but of every other Kind of the *Britiſh* Poetry; which is none of the meaneſt Branches of the *Britiſh* Learning, depends upon the Stage, and conſequently the Honour of *Great Britain* in ſome meaſure depends upon it, I humbly conceive, that the flouriſhing Condition of our Theatre is a Matter of Importance and publick Concern, and not unworthy the Conſideration of the greateſt Men in the State.

Since Dramatick Poetry was firſt introduced into *England*, it never was ſunk ſo deplorably low as it is at preſent, and every other Branch of Poetry is declined proportionably; I mean as far as it has been managed by moſt of thoſe who have liſted themſelves under *Apollo's* Standard, and who engage for their Pay. That little that has appeared that

has

Minifters together. From the very building of *London*, to the erecting the firft Theatre in it, which Time contains about thirty Centuries, we had but two *Britifh* Poets who deferve to be read : But from the Eftablifhment of our Theatres to the prefent Time, which contains fcarce a Century and a half, we may boldly affirm, that more than ten times that Number of Poets have appear'd and flourifh'd in *England*.

And here, *Sir*, I beg Leave to obferve the Advantage of Genius that *Great Britain* has over *France* with Relation to the Drama : For our Neighbours the *French*, notwithftanding the vaft Encouragement that was given by Cardinal *Richlieu*, and by *Lewis* the XIVth, at the Inftigation of Monfieur *Colbert* his Firft Minifter, never could with Juftice boaft of more than one Comick and two Tragick Poets ; whereas more than ten of our Countrymen, have, without any publick Encouragement but what they derived from the Stage itfelf (and that, how inconfiderable !) fignalized themfelves in Comedy alone, within the Compafs of thofe fifty Years that followed the Reftoration.

I know, indeed, very well, *Sir*, that other Reafons may be affigned, befides the Want of a Theatre, why no more Poets flourifhed before Queen *Elizabeth*'s Time. But I am at the fame Time convinced, that the Reafon why we have had fo many fince, has been the Eftablifhment of our Theatres. For the Dramatick Poets, the Cafe is plain, few would have given themfelves the Trouble to write Dramatick Poems, if there had not been Theatres in which they might be acted. And fome, who were by Nature qualified to fucceed better in other Kinds of Poetry

than

and the other, upon publiſhing his Book upon Hereditary Right, was impriſon'd for High Treaſon.

But, *Sir*, the following Treatiſe was likewiſe deſign'd in Defence of all the People of Quality of both Sexes in *England*, and of all the People in any Country throughout the Chriſtian World, where they frequent any Theatres ; all which numerous People he has very charitably given to the Devil to 'have and to hold for ever.

> *Nor Engine nor Device Polemick,*
> *Diſeaſe nor Doctor Epedemic,*
> *E'er ſent ſo vaſt a Colony*
> *To the infernal World as he.*

But all that I have been able to do in the Defence of ſo good a Cauſe, is to ſhew, that I heartily wiſh well to it. It belongs to you, *Sir*, and to thoſe few who reſemble you, who have Diſcernment and Taſte, that qualify you to determine ſurely, and Honour and Juſtice enough to engage you to pronounce and judge impartially, to take the *Britiſh* Drama into your Protection and Patronage, in order to retrieve its former Luſtre, and augment its Glory.

By taking the *Britiſh* Theatre into your Protection and Patronage, you would protect and patronize every other Branch of the *Britiſh* Poetry. For as the *Britiſh* Theatre, as long as it was juſtly and judiciouſly managed among us, was the only publick Rewarder of Dramatick Poetry, ſo it has been the only chief Support and Encouragement of every other Species of that noble Art. It has cheriſh'd and inflamed the Spirit of Poetry, and raiſed a noble E-mulation among us, more than all our Kings and all our

Mini-

This wife and pious Prelate, in this very Paſſage, cen-ſures the Perſons of either Sex, who frequent lewd and prophane Plays : But he does not aſſert here, that there are no Plays but what are lewd and prophane. And he affirms, that Maſquerades are of more dangerous Conſe-quence to Virtue and Good Manners, than ev'n Plays which are prophane.

Thus, *Sir*, I have endeavour'd to ſhew, that of three of the preſent reigning Diverſions, one is cruel and bar-barous, and not at all becoming either of a Chriſtian or a civilized Nation ; the Second effeminate, wanton, and ſen-ſual; and the Third, either very unmeaning, or elſe neither moral nor chriſtian.

No Art of Man in the moſt happy Age of the moſt happy Nation, has been able to find out a publick Diver-ſion that has been reaſonable, noble, manly, and virtuous, but the Drama, when it is writ as it ought be. And yet theſe wild Enthuſiaſts, who have ſhot their Bolts againſt the Stage, have ſaid not a Word againſt the other three, which cannot be defended by the leaſt Pretence that any of them can have to Goodneſs or moral Inſtruction.

Sir, The following Treatiſe is not only a Defence of Dramatick Poetry, but of the Eſtabliſh'd Government, in the Adminiſtration of which the Wiſdom of the King has given you an illuſtrious Share, and againſt which Mr. *Law*'s Pamphlet is obliquely deſigned; as were the Writ-ings which his two Predeceſſors, *Collier* and *Bedford*, pub-liſh'd againſt the Stage. *Collier*, by his Action, and *Bed-ford*, by his other Writings, becauſe profeſs'd and declar'd Enemies to the Government : One of them abſolved an im-penitent Traytor, who died with Treaſon in his Mouth ;
and

As to the *Italian* Opera's, they are allow'd by all the impartial World to be fenfual and effeminate, compared to the genuine Drama, and a greater real Promoter of wanton and fenfual Thoughts than ever the Drama was pretended to be, becaufe too great a Part of them confifting of Soft-nefs of Sound, and of Wantonnefs of Thought, they have nothing of that good Senfe and Reafon, and that artful Contrivance which are effential to the Drama. No, you know very well, *Sir*, that good Senfe and Reafon, and every ftrict Attention to an artful Defign, are fo many natural and moral Reftraints upon wanton and fenfual Thoughts.

I now, *Sir*, defire Leave to fay fomething concerning Mafquerades, which Mr. *Law* affirms to be more innocent than the Drama, which is a frontlefs Affertion, and the very Reverfe of Reafon. I remember one of our Comick Poets obferves, that young Ladies run a greater Risk of their Reputations by being familiar with Fools, than with Men of Senfe; becaufe Fools have but one Way of paffing their Time with them : So Mafquerades having neither the Senfe of the Drama, nor the Sound of the Opera, Perfons of both Sexes may go to them either with no Defign, or with a very vile one. To which I might add the late Remark of a wife and pious Prelate, which is, *That Mafque-rades deprive Virtue and Religion of their laft Refuge, Shame*; which, fays he, *keeps Multitudes of Sinners within the Bounds of Decency, after they have broke thro' all the Ties of Principle and Confcience. But this Invention fets them free from that alfo ; being neither better nor worfe, than an Opportuntiy to fay and do there, what Virtue, Decency, and Good Manners, will not permit to be faid or done in any other Place.*

a

This

bandon'd to the Slanders and the unjuſt Accuſations of their moſt inveterate Enemies.

I appeal to you, *Sir*, if they are not idle Dreamers who believe, that a great, a powerful, and an opulent People can be without publick Diverſions ; or if it is fitting they ſhould be without them. I appeal to you, *Sir*, if a great and a brave People, by being often aſſembled and pleaſed together, will not be the more pleaſed with one another, and the more among themſelves united.

But as all Pleaſures and Diverſions, both publick and private, are barbarous or gentle, rational or ſenſual, manly or effeminate, noble or baſe and degenerate ; 'tis agreed on by all the ſenſible World, that the publick Diverſions of a free Nation, ought neither to be barbarous, nor ſenſual, nor baſe, nor effeminate ; becauſe publick Diverſions of the firſt Kind reflect Diſhonour upon a brave Nation ; and Diverſions of the other three Kinds have a natural Tendency to the introducing a general and total Corruption of Manners, which is inconſiſtent with Liberty.

The publick Diverſions which are at preſent eſtabliſh'd in *Great Britain*, are either the Combats of our modern Gladiators, or the *Italian* Opera's, or the Maſquerades, or Tragedies and Comedies, which are the only genuine legitimate Entertainments of the Stage.

As for the firſt of theſe, the Combats of our modern Gladiators, I appeal to you, *Sir*, who by travelling have had the Advantage of knowing the Sentiments and Manners of other Nations, if they are not regarded by all *Europe*, excepting our ſelves, with Horror, and eſteem'd to be neither agreeable to the Spirit of Chriſtianity, nor to the Manners of a civilized People.

As

TO THE

R<small>IGHT</small> H<small>ONOURABLE</small>

GEORGE DODINGTON, Efq;

One of the L<small>ORDS</small> C<small>OMMISSIONERS</small> of His
Majefty's Treafury.

S I R,

 HE following little Treatife is, to all Ap-
pearance, fo very a Trifle, that I fhould
not have the Affurance to addrefs it to a
Gentleman of your diftinguifh'd Rank, if
my chief Defign were not to engage you,
in order to promote the Honour of your
Country, and the Good of the learned World, to take
upon you the Protection of the *Britifh* Dramatical Mufes,
fo far at leaft as to pronounce in their Favour. 'Tis the
Senfe of all who have the Honour to be acquainted with
you, that you have a perfect Knowledge of the Merits of
the Caufe, and Ability and Authority to determine it in
the laft Appeal. The *Britifh* Dramatick Mufes make this
Requeft to you, *Sir,* who have been barbaroufly ufed both
by their Friends and their Enemies ; for by their Friends
they have been more than once poorly deferted, and a-

A 2 bandon'd

will not excuse the Diſſenters from being guilty of Schiſm. By *Thomas Bennet*, D. D. Vicar of St. *Giles's Cripplegate*. The fourth Edition. 8*vo.* 1718.

30. The Indictment, Arraigment, Tryal and Judgment at large of tweny-nine Regicides, the Murtherers of his moſt Sacred Majeſty King *Charles* the Firſt, with their Speeches. 8*vo.* 1724.

31. *The Chriſtian's Pattern:* or, A Treatiſe of the Imitatson of Jeſus Chriſt. By *Thomas à Kempis.* Engliſh'd by *George Stanhope*, D. D. The tenth Edition. 8*vo.* 1721.

32. A Verſion of the Pſalms of *David*, fitted to the Tunes read in Churches. By Sir *John Denham*, Knight of the *Bath.* 8*vo.*

33. The Religious Philoſopher: or, the right Uſe of contemplating the Works of the Creator. I. In the wonderful Structure of Animal Bodies, and in particular Man. II. In the no leſs wonderful and wiſe Formation of the Elements, and their various Effects upon Animal and Vegetable Bodies. And, III. In the moſt amazing Structure of the Heavens, with all its Furniture. Deſign'd for the Conviction of Atheiſts and Infidels. By that Learned Mathematician, Dr. *Nieuwentyt.* To which is prefix'd a Letter to the Tranſlator, by the Reverend *J. T. Deſagulier*, L. L. D. F. R. S. The third Edition. Adorn'd with Cuts. 2 Vol. 4*to.* 1724.

34. The Religion of Nature delineated. The fourth Edition. 4*to.* 1726.

35. An Analytick Treatiſe of Conick Sections, and their Uſe for reſolving of Equations in determinate and indeterminate Problems. Being the Poſthumous Work of the Marquis *De L'Hoſpital.* 4*to.* 1723.

36. A Commentary upon the Prophecy and Lamentations of *Jeremiah.* By *W. Lowth*, B. D. 4*to.*

37. A Chronological Eſſay on the Ninth Chapter of the Book of *Daniel:* or, an Interpretation of the Prophecy of the ſeventy Weeks, whereby the *Jews*, in and for above 460 Years before our Saviour's Time, might certainly know the very Year in which the Meſſias was to come. By *Peter Lancaſter*, Vicar of *Bowden* in *Cheſhire*, and ſometime Student of *Chriſt-Church* in *Oxford.* 4*to.* 1722.

Lately publiſh'd for March 1726. (*being the* 15*th.*)

New Memoirs of Literature, containing an Account of new Books printed both at Home and Abroad; with Diſſertations upon ſeveral Subjects, miſcellancous Obſervations, &c. N. B. Theſe Memoirs will be publiſh'd every Month. Price 1 *s.* each.

20. A Practical Discourse concerning the great Duty of Prayer. By *Richard Crossinge*, B. D. Fellow of *Pembroke-Hall* in *Cambridge*. 8*vo.* 1720.

21. ———A Practical Discourse concerning the great Duty of Charity. 8*vo.* 1720.

22. The devout Soul, or Entertainment for a Penitent, consisting of Meditations, Poems, Hymns and Prayers, in two Parts. By *Tho. Coney*, D. D. Prebendary of *Wells*, and Rector of *Chedzey* in *Somersetshire*. 8*vo.* 1722.

23. Primitive Morality: or, the Spiritual Homilies of St. *Macarius* the *Egyptian*, full of very profitable Instructions concerning that Perfection which is expected from Christians, and which is their Duty to endeavour after. Done out of *Greek* into *English*, with several considerable Emendations, and some Enlargements from a *Bodleian* Manuscript, never before printed. 8*vo.* 1721.

24. Dr. *Lucas's* Enquiry after Happiness. In three Parts. 1. Of the Possibility of obtaining Happiness. 2. Of the true Notion of human Life. 3. Of Religious Perfection. In two Vols. The fifth Edition. 8*vo.* 1717.

25. Twenty four Sermons preach'd on several Occasions. In two Vols. By *Richard Lucas*, D. D. The second Edition.

26. *Physico-Theology:* or, a Demonstration of the Being and Attributes of God from his Works of Creation, being the Substance of sixteen Sermons preach'd in St. *Mary-le-Bow* Church, *London*, at the Honourable Mr. *Boyle's* Lectures, in the Years 1711 and 1712, with large Notes, and many curious Observations. By *W. Derham*, Canon of *Windsor*, Rector of *Upminster* in *Essex*, and F. R. S. The sixth Edition. 8*vo.* 1723.

27. *Astro-Theology:* or, a Demonstration of the Being and Attributes of God, from a Survey of the Heavens. Illustrated with Copper Plates. The fifth Edition, 8*vo.* 1725.

28. A Defence of the Validity of the *English* Ordinations, and of the Succession of the Bishops in the Church of *England:* Together with Proofs, justifying the Facts advanced in this Treatise. Written in *French* by the Reverend Father, *Peter Francis Le Courayer*, Canon Regular and Librarian of St. *Genevieve* at *Paris*. To which is prefixed, a Letter of the Author to the Translator. 8*vo.* 1725.

29. A Discourse of Schism; shewing, I. What is meant by Schism. II. That Schism is a damnable Sin. III. That there is a Schism between the Establish'd Church of *England*, and the Dissenters. IV. That this Schism is to be charg'd on the Dissenter's Side. V. That the Modern Pretences of Toleration, Agreements in Fundamentals, &*c.*
will

BOOKS printed for W. and J. INNYS.

10. Fourteen Difcourfes preached on feveral Occafions, by *William Shorey*, A. M. Lecturer of St. *Lawrence-Jewry*. 8vo. 1725.

11. Directions, Counfels and Cautions, tending to prudent Management of Affairs in common Life. Collected by *Thomas Fuller*, M. D. 120. 1725.

12. An Addrefs to Parents, fhewing them the Obligations they are under to take care of the Chriftian Education of their Children, and laying before them the principal Points in which they ought to inftruct them. By *Jofeph Hoole*, Vicar of *Haxey*. 8vo. 1724.

13. Three Dialogues between *Hylas* and *Philonous*. The Defign of which is plainly to demonftrate the Reality and Perfections of human Knowledge; the incorporeal Nature of the Soul, and the immediate Providence of a Deity, in oppofition to Scepticks and Atheifts. Alfo to open a Method for rendring the Sciences more eafy, ufeful and compendious. By *George Berkley*, M. A. Fellow of *Trinity* College, *Dublin*. The fecond Edition. 8vo. 1725.

14. Pious Thoughts concerning the Knowledge and Love of God, and other holy Exercifes. By the late Archbifhop of *Cambray*; together with a Letter of Chriftian Inftruction, by a Lady, done out of *French*. 8vo. 1720.

15. A Difcourfe of the Truth and Certainty of Natural Religion, and the indifpenfible Obligations to Religious Worfhip, from Nature and Reafon. In two Books. By *David Martin*, late Paftor of the *French* Church at *Utrecht*. Tranflated from the *French*. The fecond Edition. 8vo. 1725.

16. The Beauty of Holinefs in the Common-Prayer, as fet forth in four Sermons, preach'd at the *Rolls* Chapel in the Year 1716. The eighth Edition. To which is added, a *Rationale* on Cathedral Worfhip, or Choir Service. The fecond Edition. By *Thomas Biffe*, D. D. 8vo. 1721.

17. Decency and Order in publick Worfhip, recommended in three Difcourfes preach'd in the Cathedral Church of *Hereford*. By *Thomas Biffe*, D. D. Chancellor of the faid Church. 8vo. 1723.

18. Eight Sermons preach'd at the Cathedral Church of St. *Paul*'s in Defence of the Divinity of our Lord Jefus Chrift; upon the Encouragement given by the Lady *Moyer*, and at the Appointment of the Lord Bifhop of *London*, &c. By *Daniel Waterland*, D. D. Mafter of *Magdalen* College in *Cambridge*. The fecond Edition. 8vo. 1720.

19. Dr. *Mangey*'s Practical Difcourfes upon the Lord's Prayer, preach'd before the Honourable Society of *Lincoln's-Inn*. The third Edition. 8vo. 1721.

23. A

BOOKS *Printed for* W. *and* J. INNYS, *at the West End of* St. Paul's. 1726.

LAW OUTLAW'D:

Or, A SHORT

REPLY

TO

Mr. *Law's* Long DECLAMATION against the STAGE

WHEREIN

The Wild Rant, Blind Paſſion, and Falſe Rea‑
ſoning of that Piping-hot PHARISEE are
made apparent to the meaneſt Capacity.

Together with.

An Humble PETITION to the Governours
of the *Incurable Ward* of *Bethlehem* to take pity
on the poor diſtracted Authors of the Town, and
not ſuffer 'em to terrify Mankind at this rate.

Written at the Requeſt of the Orange‑Women, *and
for the* Publick Good, *by the impartial Pen of
Mrs. S——O——, a Lover of both Houſes.*

L O N D O N,

Printed for the Benefit of the *Candle-Snuffers,* and ſold by
the *Bookſellers* of *London* and *Weſtminſter.* 1726.
(Price Four Pence.)

A SHORT
REPLY
TO
Mr. *L A W.*

EN of Caprice and Whim may be indulg'd in particular Humours so long as they are not mischievous. It is a Compliment the well bred part of Mankind pay to Madmen and Children, not to contradict them in their little Oddnesses ; but when they grow troublesome, and presume too far on the World's Indul-

gence,

gence, it is fit they fhould be fnubb'd and con-
troul'd.

This is the Cafe between me and my Antagonift ; had he never appear'd in Print, I had left
the *Tartuffe* to himfelf, and he might have fnuf-
fled againft the Stage to this Day unmolefted, but
when he prefumes thus publickly to libel and de-
fame my favourite Diverfion, he is infupporta-
ble; nor fhall I fuffer the *Wall-Eyed* Hypocrite
to pafs unchaftifed.

This Man, of a Temper abftracted from all
that's gay and generous, looks with an evil Eye
on the innocent Diverfions of other People, and,
like fome of the old primitive Puritans, cannot
bear to fee any body merry. He would have all
Mankind come into his gloomy rigid way of
thinking ; and is fo pofitive of being in the
right, that he tells us his Arguments againft the
Stage are as ftrong and plain as any that can
be urged againft the Worfhip of Images ; when,
alas, if Image-Worfhip had not found more
powerful Antagonifts than the Stage has of Mr.
Law, we had all kifs'd the Pope's Toe to this
Day.

For,

For, begging Mr. *Law's* Pardon, I cannot come into his way of arguing. He firſt begs the Queſtion, and then takes it for granted. Having thus palmed his own Aſſertion upon his Readers, he very modeſtly draws his own Inferences, and remains, as he imagines unanſwerable : But I muſt confeſs I think far otherwiſe ; I never read a more unfair Reaſoner, his Arguments are ſtrained beyond the pitch of Truth ; they are too chimerical to have any effect on thinking People ; and are only calculated to terrify Perſons whoſe Conſciences and Capacities are feeble and tender.

Theſe he frightens with *Bull-beggars* and *Raw-head* and *Bloodybones*, tells 'em a long *Rig-may-Roll* of dancing Devils and ſinging Devils; of the Devil's Ground, the Devil's Houſe, and the Devil and all : Surely the Devil and he are great Cronies, the Word Devil being in almoſt every other Line of his Book. But let thoſe be ſcar'd with his *Bugbears* who fear the Devil ; for my part I defy him and all his Works, of which *Law's* Book is no ſmall part, being written at his Inſtigation.

For

For who but a Man of a devilish Temper,
puff'd up with a superftitious Self-fufficiency, and
blinded with the Madnefs of falfe Zeal, would
have flown in the Face of the Government, and
thus publickly affronted all Mankind. Is it not
enough for him he is indulg'd in his own Whims,
but he muft dart his oblique Reflections againft
his Superiours, and that in fo fcandalous, fo vile
a Manner ?

In his ninth Page he tells us 'tis as unlawful
to go to a Play as to affift and reward a Man for
renouncing a Chriftian Life ; and that to approve, affift, or encourage a Player, is as evidently finful as to encourage a Man in ftealing.
That Players are as bad as Thieves and Murderers ; and, That the Bufinefs of a Player
(*Pag.* 10.) is one of the moft abominable of
Crimes.

If fo, why are not the Players hang'd as
well as Thieves and Murderers ? and why are
they conniv'd at in the moft abominable of
Crimes ? and why are not their Encouragers
and Abettors taken out of the Pit, Boxes, &c.
and brought to condign Punifhment ?

This

This is what he drives at; nor dare I draw the Inference he fo artfully infinuates-- ---But I deny his every Affertion, and affirm to his teeth, that,

I. The Bufinefs of a Player is fo far, from being the moft abominable of Crimes, it is repugnant neither to divine or human Law.

II. That Perfons may go to hear Plays, and not be guilty of Crimes equivalent to Murder, Theft, &c.

III. That Mr. *Law* is more guilty than Players or their Audiences.

My firft Affertion may be eafily proved, there being no particular Text of Scripture againft Players or Playhoufes; nor is there any Allufion that can carry the leaft Hint that way: Now we may very juftly prefume that if our Saviour had efteem'd Playhoufes or Players pernicious, they had been fpecify'd in his Doctrines, which are doubtlefs the whole Summary of the new Law, and never efcap'd his particular Notice, efpecially when in his time there was a moft magnificent Theatre in *Jerufalem*; but, far from that, he he chofe rather to lafh fuch Hypocrites as *Law*, and cry, *Wo unto you* Scribes *and* Pharifees, &c. *Mat.* xxiii. 14----29.

I muft entreat the Reader to turn to this Chapter, and he will find in that moft excellent Denunciation the Picture of my Antagonift moft exactly drawn ; our Saviour's exprefs Words being fo fevere a Satire upon fuch *Pharifees*, that he needs no other Confutation, and if he has any Grace or Shame left, his Mouth muft be ftopt, and himfelf acknowledge his own Impertinence.

I fhall pafs over St. *Paul's* Quotation from *Menander*, and many other Authorities I could produce in Vindication of the Stage, having, as I humbly prefume, fairly confuted his firft Propofition, upon which his whole whimfical Syftem is founded.

As for human Laws, ever fince there have been Players and Playhoufes in *England*, they have been under the immediate Protection and Encouragement of the Government, a number of them at this prefent time being fworn into his Majefty's actual Service, under the Title of *His Majefty's Company of* C O M E D I A N S : If fo, how impudent is *Law* to compare fuch Perfons with Thieves,

Thieves, &c. and at the fame time to make their Encouragers as bad as themfelves ? I leave his moft unmannerly, unjuft, and difloyal Conclufion to Imagination, as not fit to flow from the Pen of a Subject or a Chriftian.

It is evident, the Royal Family, the Nobility, and, in a word, the Chief of the *Englifh* Nation have been at Plays; nay, fome Men of Learning and Probity much fuperiour to **Mr.** *Law* have wrote Plays; and others as good Chriftians and as ftrict Livers as Mr. *Law* have acted Plays : I dare oppofe Mr. *Wilks*, Mr. *Mills*; and feveral other Actors, in their private Characters, to Mr. *Law*, or any other canting Hypocrite whatever. If Players are fuch Reprobates, why are they admitted to the Sacrament, or even into the Church ? But Mr. *Law* not only arraigns the Legiflature, but the Clergy for not coming into his whimfical Notions.

Since therefore Theatres are not contrary to divine or human Laws, what muft we think of this Madman, who rails at Theatres till he foams again. But his own Words are his beft Condemnation. He exclaims againft perfonating,

B   or

or drawing Characters, and yet himself draws three Characters under the borrow'd Names of *Lovis*, *Trebonia*, and *Jucunda*. This is the very Sin he cries out against, yet cannot see the Beam in his own Eye. But I shall set him in a right light, and from direct Quotations furnish the Town with a little Comedy written by this Puritan, which I shall call, *The* BRITISH TARTUFFE : *Or*, *The* LUNATICK ZEALOT : And which I hope to get acted the Beginning of the Winter. Till when I humbly take leave of the Town, and remain

Their Humble Servant,

S. O

To

To the Worſhipful the Governours of the incurable Ward of *Beth-lehem.*

The Humble PETITION *of ſeveral Hundreds of Merchants, Shopkeepers, and other Inhabitants paying Scot and Lot, in the Cities of* London *and* Weſtminſter,

SHEWETH,

THAT your Petitioners cannot without great Grief of Mind behold the poor diſtracted Authors of the Town running thro' the publick Streets. Some haring and ſtaring, with Looks and Actions wild as ſavage Creatures, over-run our Children, overturn our Wares, break our Show-boards, beat down the perambulating Venders of Fruit, Fiſh, &c. and ſcatter their Goods about the Streets. Others, with Eyes fix'd to the Ground, muttering to themſelves,

ſelves,

felves, regardlefs of Danger, put us in the utmoft pain, out of mere Pity for our Fellow-Creatures, whom we expect every Minute to be run over by Coaches, Carts, Drays, &c. whofe Drivers know no Mercy. It is a piteous Sight to fee thefe poor unhappy Wretches beating, bruifing, and ftunning themfelves, by running full-butt againft Pofts, Pumps, &c. by tumbling Head-foremoft into Cellars, Vaults, &c. to the endangering their Necks, and the Terror of all Spectators who have the leaft Humanity. And what is worfe, thefe poor Wretches infatuate our Youth with the contagious Spirit of Poetry, infomuch that our Book-keepers, Apprentices, &c.. are making Verfes, when they fhould be about our Bufinefs. Even thofe who write not themfelves, fpend half their time in reading Legends, Romances, Plays, Poems, and Pamphlets, to the great detriment of Trade, and Prejudice of the Publick.

We therefore recommend to your Charity a diftracted Clerk lately come from *Ireland*, who runs up and down the Streets, crying *Pudding and Dumpling ! Pudding and Dumpling !* which Cry fends all our young People directly to the Cupboard, infomuch that we are in a manner eat out of Houfe and Home.

The

The next Object is poor *Mad Bess,* who in
a romantic manner calls herself E L I Z A. This
unhappy Gentlewoman is run diftracted with
Legends, Romances, and Adventures, and has
the *Cacoethes Scribendi* fo ftrong upon her, that if
due care be not timely taken, the poor Creature will certainly write herfelf to Death.

The next Object is a little fat *Sonnetteer,* who
who went mad for the Love of *Sally in our Al-
ley.* This poor Soul runs up and down wild
from one End of the Town to the other, fing-
ing and fmiling to himfelf, and cannot fee a
Card but he'll make a Song upon it. He is a
walking Library, carrying always a Porter's Load
of Mufic Books; infomuch that what with his
Burdens, what with his Fat, and what with
his violent Motion in walking, he will certainly
fry himfelf to death before *Midfummer,* if he is
not taken in.

There is likewife one *Hillarius,* a Gentleman-
like fort of Man, but as mad as a *March* Hare
(the more the Pity.) He is a *Plain-Dealer,* and
fcruples not to tell every one their own, and ought
therefore to be fecur'd, Truth not being to be
fpoken at all times.

We

We muſt likewiſe recommend a poor diſtracted *Caledonian* Phyſician as a fit Object of your Charity. This unhappy Creature fancies himſelf a Prophet, and gives out Warnings of a *Tear of Wonders*, of *white Bears*, and *wild Men*, to the Terror and Amazement of his Majeſty's liege Subjects.

But above all we beg you to take immediately into your Care a poor lunatick Maſter of Arts, who raves like a Madman, preaching D——n to all Mankind, eſpecially ſuch who go to Plays, Opera's, or other theatrical Entertainments. This Man writes without Fear or Wit, and what is worſe, finds out Perſons as mad as himſelf to print what he writes; ſo that if he is not immediately taken care of, we ſhall certainly be overrun with Pamphlets, eſpecially if he ſhould follow the Example of ſome late Writers, and anſwer his own Works,

We could offer numberleſs other Objects of Compaſſion; Poets, Politicians, Projectors, Painters, Muſicians, Stockjobbers, &c. but well knowing that all the Hoſpitals in *London* cannot contain them, we wait with Patience till the Legiſlature ſhall make proper Proviſion.

We

We are but too apprehenſive this well intended Petition will meet with great Oppoſition from certain Printers and Stationers, as alſo from Paſtry-Cooks, Trunk-Makers, and other Dealers in Waſte-Paper; but we hope the Publick Good will over-rule all private Advantage, and that your Worſhips, in your great Wiſdom and Compaſſion, will take pity on theſe poor miſerable Objeƈts, which will very much conduce to the publick Tranquillity.

And Your Petitioners ſhall ever pray.

F I N I S.

L. O N D O N, Printed for *A. Moore* near St. *Paul's.* 1726.